LIBRARY AUTOMATION
AS A SOURCE OF
MANAGEMENT INFORMATION

Papers presented at the 1982 Clinic on Library Applications
of Data Processing, April 25-28, 1982

Clinic on Library Applications
of Data Processing: 1982

Library Automation
as a Source of
Management Information

Edited by
F. WILFRID LANCASTER

Graduate School of Library and Information Science
University of Illinois at Urbana-Champaign

Library of Congress Cataloging in Publication Data 84 -27

Clinic on Library Applications of Data Processing (19th :
    1982 : University of Illinois at Urbana-Champaign)
    Library automation as a source of management infor-
mation.

    "Papers presented at the 1982 Clinic on Library
Applications of Data Processing, April 25-28, 1982"—Half
title p.
    Includes index.
    1. Library administration—Data processing—Con-
gresses. 2. Libraries—Automation—Congresses.
3. Library science—Data processing—Congresses.
I. Lancaster, F. Wilfrid. II. University of Illinois at
Urbana-Champaign. Graduate School of Library and
Information Science III. Title.
Z678.C63   1982   025.3'028'54   83-9110
ISBN: 0-87845-068-8

CONTENTS

Introduction

The nineteenth annual Clinic on Library Applications of Data Processing was held at the Illini Union, University of Illinois, April 25-28, 1982.

In the last twenty years, two of the most significant developments in the library field have been the increase in the adoption of automated procedures and growing interest in the measurement and evaluation of library services. Yet, the marriage of these two trends—that is, the use of automated systems as sources of data to permit improved management and decision-making—has not been a major focus of professional interest. The 1982 clinic sought to correct this situation by focusing attention on the management information component of automated systems in libraries. As far as the organizers are aware, this was the first conference to deal in toto with this particular topic.

The papers reproduced here represent great variety ranging from a tutorial on management information and decision support systems (Boland), through more philosophical discussions (Heim, Olsgaard and Shank) on the value to the library manager of computer-derived information, to studies of the use of automated systems as sources of management data in libraries and information services of various types (Brownrigg, Caldwell, Dowlin, Evans, Jacob/Kaske, Kennedy, Mullin).

This volume, we believe, contributes a significant body of literature on an important topic that has received little previous attention in the library profession.

F.W. LANCASTER
Editor

RUSSELL SHANK
University Librarian and Professor
University of California at Los Angeles

Management, Information and the Organization: Homily from the Experience of the Data Rich but Information Poor

Calvin Mooers's Law has long been one of my favorites. I often use it as an excuse for irrational behavior in library management. Over twenty years ago, Calvin Mooers commented: "An information retrieval system will tend *not* to be used whenever it is more painful and troublesome for a customer to have information than for him not to have it."[1]

Mooers was involved with information storage and retrieval systems in science, but his words are just as appropriate for management information systems (MIS). The problem with having information in Mooer's view is that you can't just let it sit there if it indicates that something must be done. If that something is hard to do or involves difficult social consequences (such as disrupting the faculty's habits of library use, or the student's timing of meeting his date), it will only cause ulcers, sleepless nights or unemployment if you don't make the adjustment. Of course there is one way to avoid all of the trouble, and that is not to have the information in the first place.

If Mooers's Law is right, then managers and administrators should reject management information systems. Yet here one is, deliberating positively on the future of such systems presumably enhanced to new levels of capabilities by the computer. Well, I suppose that's all right, for in spite of Mooers's Law or anything I might say, human nature makes one inquisitive so that counting things and arraying the tally in various displays comes with his genes.

But Mooers's Law alone is not sufficient. I have discovered Russell's inference: "If there are two things to be counted, that which is the easiest will cost the most to tally." Then there is Shank's syndrome: "If you count one of two things the boss will want the other." This is followed closely by the invariable derivation: "That which the boss wants is the most ambiguous to define, the most expensive to count, but the most relevant to him." And we have the petulant ukase: Never wait for the information—do it now and then gather data to prove you had the right idea but the "system" subverted the purity of your solution and for irrelevant reasons. Or the invariable proposition: The sum of the columns is never equal to the sum of the footings. Or the perfect postulate: Don't just stand there—count!

Why do we collect data which can be turned into management information? Well, there can be many reasons:

1. The data *might* be worth something. The choice of tasks among several alternatives for the use of one's time, assuming that the utility of the alternatives is the same, might be clearly indicated by the data which shows how much resource would be required to perform each task.

2. We collect some data to sustain tradition. For fifty years research libraries have been reporting the size of their holdings and it has now become a ritual to contribute to the ARL census. Some await the report eagerly which year by year shows them bobbing up and down amongst their peers in a variety of measurable elements. About the best I can say of it is that it might sustain some ego gratification. Unless one is a Harvard graduate there is always something to aim at. Or one can take pleasure—or not—about the company he's in.

3. Some collecting is done just because the data is there. It is human nature to sort things into piles, and to wander idly over the field counting things as one goes.

4. Some data is collected so as to avoid embarrassment. Someone might ask questions about the operations which can best be answered with numbers. What manager would be considered qualified for the job if he or she couldn't tell how much of anything goes into or comes out of the operation. There is, of course, a certain peace of mind which is derived from collecting data, even if no one ever asks about it. At least one has data which can be used in press releases.

5. There is, of course, the great public demand for accountability. Since most of the public does not have the faith any more to believe the litanies of those who spend public money, they need data to explain the use of public money. We may snow them with numbers, but at least the appearance of precision on our part will give the appearance that we think we know what we are doing—and we're doing it for them!

6. Sometimes data is collected in order to create tables and reports to overwhelm the administration. Perhaps this is just another form of accountability. But busy administrators don't need more information (which by the way might be accurate and painful to deal with). What one actually finds is that less and less data is forwarded through the organization

since less and less is read or heeded. From one standpoint, therefore, the function of an organization seems to be to suppress data. What is often lacking is a distinction between data which contains information to control processes at the local level, and data which explains the reason for, or the need for, decisions on resource allocation to the next level. The same data does not always provide the foundation for the extraction of information needed at each level. Hence the need to stratify the management information system to match the management levels in an organization. This would tend to make the notion of a standard set of data to be gathered for the whole organization irrational. Furthermore, the higher one goes in an organization, the more difficult it is to predict what issues have to be handled, hence the more difficult it is to predict management's need for information.

7. Data is collected so that those who give it—those who are doing the work—think that managers know what's going on and care. There are many signals which can be given after they get the data which will sustain this impression. Part of the art of management is giving signals.

8. Data is collected because we cannot lose by doing it. Institutions assess no penalties on departments—including management information departments—for collecting too much data. Data gathering is seldom priced, hence the evaluation of management information systems is seldom based on the economics of running the systems. Management requires data which it assumes can be gathered easily in the course of doing the tasks being counted, and that takes us back to the human nature theory of data gathering.

Just as there is no penalty for collecting too much data, there is no premium on brevity of data collection. Information management departments or systems are not judged on the basis of the value of the decisions which could be based on the information in the data they gather. Managers further up in the hierarchy are judged on the quality of their decisions, which could *possibly* be based on information from a management information system, but which does not necessarily need to be. The whole system seems to be put into place as a perpetual motion machine all too often installed without there being any analysis of what to do with the data.

Now for any and all of these reasons, and probably more, we collect and report data. But a typical administrative characteristic seems to be the appearance of ignoring irrefutable information derived from good data. This is particularly true in the political arena. There the black and white of logic is overwhelmed by back scratching and other heuristic devices. Most of our political and some of our administrative behavior seems to be based on a sample of one—preferably apocryphal—incident.

If we are so good why is our data rejected up the line? My inventory of reasons is long and sound, based on many years both as a producer of data about operations, and as a manager whose primary functions seems to be finding reasons why managers, administrators and politicians reject data. This may occur because:

1. It is not clear what, if anything, can be done about whatever the data purports to show. Here I have reworded Mooers's Law. Management information will be rejected to the extent that it indicates that something has to be done. Fewer managers have been fired for doing *nothing* than for trying *something*.
2. Rejection may occur because the data is not trusted. One way to reject a whole report is to find one error in it. This error can be used to discredit the whole report. Then the difficult decision can be avoided with impugnity.
3. Rejection may occur if it is not clear if the data indicates something good or something bad. Clear data, and good information, does little to clarify ambiguous social conditions.
4. A corollary to the previous pronouncement is that data is rejected because those who present it do not have the theatrical skills required to convince the hierarchy that it means anything.
5. Data is rejected because the recipient of the information is inclined to see "the other side" of the issue. This is the side for which one did not gather data. This is particularly true of social and political issues. The use of this technique is one of the signs of the successful politician or administrator.
6. Rejection may occur because the recipient has his own MIS which produces contrary data, or provides grounds for alternate inferences. This produces enough ambiguity so that the manager or politican can display the wisdom of quick, seat-of-the-pants judgment. If the person has been successful to date (that's why he or she is in the management position), he or she will probably be right again.
7. Data is rejected because there is no way to match the data from different but related departments or situations. This moves us again into the arena of ambiguity and the need for a carefully designed, stratified management information system.
8. Data rejection occurs because there is a lack of understanding along the way as to what data and information will sustain decisions about the value of services. This is either the result of a manager's inability to direct the enterprise by thinking of scenarios for a possible future, or a lack of empathy for the manager's problems by those down the line. Lack of empathy may short-circuit as many upwardly mobile people as it does the data they provide.

Perhaps I can be a bit more sanguine about management information systems with the involvement of computers. Obviously if data storage and retrieval is the name of the game, computers are ideally suited to this function. They can tally and summarize and they can work fast. If the summaries can be made hierarchical, just like the organization, then computers can take over the screening (or data suppression) function but with a difference. With a computer and the right software, the manager can get not only his or her own compressed summary data, but at any time go into the file and see anyone's data should the fancy strike him.

But I worry. Data system operators tell me that the cost of storage is coming down rapidly—has been for years. What this means is that it will not cost so much on a unit basis to store the garbage; so for the money, we can store more. But all that we will then have is cheaper garbage.

Computers have still another advantage. They can count the transactions as they work on them. No longer does someone have to tally the number of circulation cards at the end of the day, or the orders sent out, or the number of items processed. Programmed correctly, the computer will do the counting as it goes. Just look at the number on the bottom line. If nothing else, this is a labor saver.

To me the chief advantage of the computer, though, is that it can economically work on the "what if" questions. These are the ones that managers like to ask, but usually cannot get answered because there is no way to test all of the variables in order to substantiate answers without operating on the patient (the library or its users) without an anesthetic.

The "what if" questions I am thinking of are operational. Administrators may ponder notions such as: What if we closed seven of the branches two hours earlier each day, paid the staff to travel to a regional installation for the remaining time, beefed up the reference staff for half the hours lost, and added 25 percent to the budget of the book delivery system? What would be the differential cost (excess or saved), and what would be the effect on service (given some reasonable measures of service output of the library)? This is not the kind of question that can be answered with assurance. The hot, highly successful managers might be able to handle it. After all, they are hot and highly successful because they have the intuition, the experience, or the ability to make their analyses sound good, which leads them to answer questions while dodging issues.

But in the main they tread gingerly—take one step at a time—try to find those things which can be done relatively cheaply, and which do not involve an intolerable sunk cost. If we have to retreat we at least want to do it gracefully and cheaply.

The computer could handle all of the data for the mix of options we would like to test *if only*. And here is the crux of the issue of making the computer a real management ally. One could do it best *if only* he had good models of the library as an operating organism, and lots of data about the units of operation in the system. Then he could run libraries as models with different variables, look at paper outputs and do it all without disturbing current operations. Then one could make decisions—if he had confidence and a lot of courage. Intuition and experience might still be the *sine qua non* of the administrator, but now the data output by the management information system would be in the context of the management questions.

Modeling and collecting a large volume of operational data would then make some sense. The work of people such as Hamburg, Kantor and King are steps in this direction. So is that of those who have done the many user studies. But their work only provides proofs of the utility of the process. They show the way to analyze problems and to count data. What we need to do now is to build models of library operations. And the data to be inserted in them must be specific to the library being analyzed. But beware of the monster we might create. According to the *Wall Street Journal* the major computer centers in the United States produced over 240 billion pages of printout in 1980—about 1000 pages for every man, woman and child. This number could grow to 10,000 pages per person by 1985 at the rate we are going.[2]

Wildavsky said that: "Alas, access to data does not automatically convert itself into information. Inference and interpretation are required."[3] This is where administrative talent (whether based on intuition or experience) must come to the fore. It cannot be replaced by the computer. It could even be stymied by receiving thousands of pages, or even thousands of lines, of data. Even computer graphics which coordinate and display data in compact and different ways might not help. Some users are visually illiterate. Here it may be well to note an even deeper issue. Not only is there widespread visual illiteracy, but also there may be an even greater antipathy—if not illiteracy—to mathematics. If computers lead to an increase in quantitative reports we might expect an even greater rejection of the output of MIS by administrators and politicians. Unless we can improve peoples' ability in general to handle numbers, the rejection syndrome is likely to be reinforced.

Areas for concern when the computer is brought into MIS abound. While the data storage costs per bit are coming down rapidly, Parkinson's Law prevails. Data will expand to fill storage space—and the total cost of the system will go up both because it costs a lot to collect all of the data that can be stored, and because the actual cost of the storage mechanism goes up even though it densely packs in a lot more data with each machine generation.

Both the power of the computer and the cost of using it might force us at last to pay the kind of attention to management information systems and

problems that has been notably lacking in our profession. We are
extremely cost conscious in every other aspect of library work. We establish
budgets for various phases of our operations. We seldom do it, however, for
management information systems. Budgets for management information
ought to be developed, and done so on the basis of the utility of the
information the systems can extract and give out. Or perhaps managers
should be given information budgets—either in terms of cash they can
transfer to the management information system, or cash they can give for
information, or in terms of the time they are allowed to spend examining
data and information. (In a way, most administrators have a time budget.
Some management information systems output is rejected simply because
managers are enervated by merely seeing a pile of printout and wondering
where they will get the time to look at it.)

At last we may have the impetus to place heavier emphasis on the
education of managers to analyze and state issues in terms which will
suggest their information needs. And perhaps we can even learn to evaluate
administrators and managers for their ability to state issues and to make
inferences based on sound information derived from reliable and sensible
data. In this realm we are asking people to live symbolically. George Miller
of Princeton warns that: "More and more people will become useless if
they cannot live at the symbolic level."[4] The success of computer modeling, therefore, might well be proportional to the ability to live
symbolically.

We must, of course, recognize that the high technology of computers
does not mean that they are infallible. That is—and this ought to be
obvious from what I have said so far—people, not computers, solve problems. Neat columns, multi-inverted matrices, accurate tallies, quick eating
and consolidation of lots of data are not substitutes for intuition and
inference.

In case you missed it, here's where I have been. As a manager I am not
overwhelmingly enthusiastic about the utility of management information systems—up to now. I am skeptical about why we count, and I am not
certain we can see the way to use information derived from the data. We
have created reasons—or perhaps just allowed human nature to take its
course—to reject data. The computer, however, might finally get us nearer
Nirvana in the management information arena. A big task for the profession is to find ways to let the computer stimulate the organization under
different circumstances. Then maybe the manager's knowledge and intuition will be supported with something more than faith.

But there is still work to do. The computer has to be fed and kept on
the right track. We could fail. I think of the story of the two men who were
cast adrift in a life boat in the cold North Atlantic Ocean. Just as they were

about to take their last breaths, one looked up and said: "Praise the Lord, we're saved. Here comes the Titanic."

ACKNOWLEDGMENT

I am indebted to Aaron Wildavsky (UC Berkeley) whose views on management information have been eloquently expressed in many places, but particularly in his unpublished paper "Information as an Organizational Problem."

REFERENCES

1. Mooers, Calvin N. "Mooers' Law, or Why Some Retrieval Systems are Used and Others are Not." *American Documentation* 11(July 1960):ii.

2. Needle, David. "Managers Face a New Problem: An Information Glut." *Infoworld* 4(1 March 1982):17.

3. Wildavsky, Aaron. "Information as an Organizational Problem." Paper presented at a colloquium sponsored by Public/Not-for-Profit Management and Computers and Information Systems Curriculum Areas, Graduate School of Management, 9 Oct. 1981, UCLA.

4. Miller, George *quoted in* Fiske, Edward B. "Schools Enter the Computer Age: An Analysis." *New York Times*, 25 April 1982, p. 38.

RICHARD J. BOLAND, JR.
Associate Professor
Department of Accountancy
University of Illinois at Urbana-Champaign

Tutorial on Management Information Systems

Introduction

Management information is communication that leads to managerial action, and managerial action is a betterment achieved through a process of planning and control. A critical distinction in discussing management information is the difference between data and information. Data are any coded messages, considered apart from their use by an individual. Information, on the other hand, is the meaning of data to an individual. Information, therefore, is derived from data through interpretation and is ultimately a subjective phenomenon available only to the individual interpreter.

The first problem in discussing management information is to resolve the issue of subjectivity so that we might proceed with the question of system design. The field of management information systems has done this by treating as information, data that have been selectively assembled and structured so that we believe they will be useful to their recipient because we can adequately anticipate the meaning that will be gained.

Thus a discussion of management information always presupposes a recipient, a context and a use. The recipient is an individual manager in an organizational context who is engaged in decision-making activity. Management information must always be considered in light of all three of these aspects:

1. The *decision situation* includes an analysis of the type of problem being addressed, the adequacy of evidence required, and the range of normative and descriptive models available for understanding how the decision is or should be made.

2. The *organizational context* includes an analysis of the structure, style, climate, and power that characterizes the organization as well as aspects of the larger culture that impact the norms of perception, cognition, evaluation, and behavior used by its members.
3. The *individual manager* includes an analysis of the limits of cognitive ability, the dynamics of group processes, and the cognitive style that characterizes the way an individual collects and processes data.

Fundamentally, therefore, a discussion of management information cannot be value free. If we are to move beyond a discussion of mere data, then we must either affirm the status quo or propose a change in the decision situation, the organizational context or the individual manager. Either way, we take a normative position with respect to these three aspects when we make a design statement about an information system.

An appreciation of the distinction between data and information leads to a second problem in discussing management information. Data, as data, have a cost; and data, as information, have a value. In general, the cost of data increases as the amount collected increases, but the value of information does not. Information has a marginal rate of return which diminishes as its quantity increases. When we discuss the use of automation to replace existing manual processes, we can identify reductions in the cost of labor, space, time, etc. to produce a given output. Cost and value calculations, though often imprecise, can be made.

However, when we move beyond using automation to process repetitive transactions at the operational level, and explore the use of automation to enhance management decision-making, our ability to quantify the value of an information system becomes very problematic. We shift away from an assessment of efficiency and quantitative improvements toward an assessment of effectiveness and qualitative improvements in the functioning of the organization.

The two problems of data versus information and cost versus value set the stage for presenting a framework for analyzing management decision-making and a process for developing information systems to support decision-making. This paper is in four sections. Section one defines the organization as a system and the manager as a decision-maker about that system. Section two applies the framework to a library as a system. Section three derives implications for information system design, and section four explores the process of system development.

A Systems View of Organization

The systems approach is a broad label for the general attempt to understand organizations by analyzing their relational and dynamic aspects. The organization is viewed as a set of relationships between component parts that stand apart from an environment, receiving inputs from it and producing outputs that are received by it. Thus the organization is an open system that is dependent on input and output relations with its environment, and organizes its internal components to meet those input and output demands.

Internally, each component of the organization is understood as the relationship between its own subunits as it receives input from, and produces output to other components of the organization or its environment. Thus, each level of analysis of the system (organization, component, subunit, etc.) is both a whole—with relations between subunits that must be maintained—and a part of a larger whole, with input and output relations between other parts of that whole.

Systems are seen as the nested, hierarchical organization of relatively self-contained sets of relationships between internal components, interacting by input/output processes with a larger environment. This view is important because it emphasizes that any "problem" with the organization must be understood in terms of its internal and external relations. It cannot be understood in isolation or out of context. Also, since organizations produce myriad outputs and are constituted by a very large number of relationships, the role of managers as active determinants of the problems they face (by defining inputs, outputs and relations of interest to them) is made apparent.

The basic building block of the system approach is the notion of input, process and output (see figure 1).

Environment

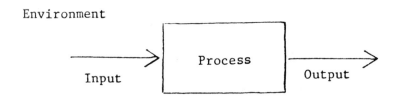

Fig. 1. Basic Input-Process-Output Model

The process can be left as an unexplained "black box," or can be expanded to include any level of detail of boxes within boxes. A very crude application to a library would be as indicated in figure 2.

As a first elaboration of this crude image, we will add the concept of levels of decision-making. The decision-maker can be viewed as making strategic, managerial or operational level decisions. At a strategic level, the

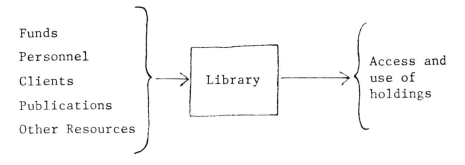

Fig. 2. Application of the Input-Process-Output Model

decision-maker is concerned with defining and prioritizing goals and objectives, and with securing the resources to achieve them. Here the manager questions and refines the basic mission of the organization— what client's are emphasized, what type and scope of services are provided, what will the character of the holdings be, what will the criteria for success and performance evaluation be?

At the managerial level, the decision-maker takes as given the resources available, the statement of mission and priorities, and the standard of performance evaluation. The problem is to arrange the operations, schedule activities, and allocate resources for the purpose of effectively achieving the strategic goals. The key idea here is effectiveness in the way the organization is configured, and the way resources are allocated.

At the operational level, the decision-maker is concerned with the details of procedures for carrying out organizational functions defined at the managerial level. Here the emphasis is on efficiency in performance, on reducing bottlenecks in flows through the system, and on removing unnecessary redundancy.

These three levels of decision-making are added to the basic input-process-output model in figure 3. Each level of decision can be further characterized by three stages of the decision-making process: intelligence, design and choice.

Intelligence. This is the initial stage of a decision process in which the manager is concerned with understanding the situation as a basis for defining the need for action or identifying the need for decision-making. The emphasis is on defining problems, threats, opportunities, and constraints that require action.

Design. At this stage, the decision-maker has identified a decision problem, and is inventing alternative courses of action and developing ideas for dealing with the problem. The recent emphasis on creativity in

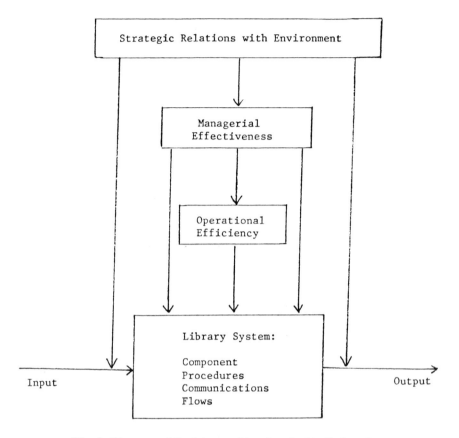

Fig. 3. Diagram of Decision-making Levels Applied to the
Basic Input-Process-Output Model

management training attests to the need for more attention to this stage of the decision process.

Choice. This stage is frequently discussed as if it comprised the whole of management decision-making. Here, a course of action is selected from the set of alternatives that have been identified for meeting the needs of the problem, as it has been defined. We can treat this process as one of pure rational choice of the best alternative, or as a satisfying choice of one that is "good enough."

These stages of decision-making are not a tidy, linear sequence of steps, but are an iterative, cyclical process in which our understanding of the situation, the alternatives we are considering, and our evaluation of those alternatives interact with each other over time. The cyclic, iterative nature of decision-making is depicted in figure 4.

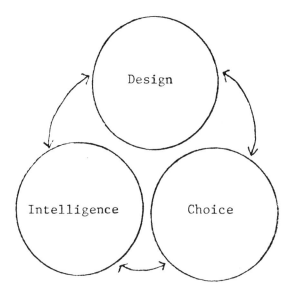

Fig. 4. Diagram of the Cycles in the Decision-making Process

Decision-making at each stage and level discussed earlier can be further characterized by the degree of "structure" they display. Structure refers to the relative ease with which we understand and accomplish the decision-making phases, and ranges from very well-structured decisions to very ill-structured ones. Well-structured decisions are those that can be fully specified such that a procedure can be designed to automate the decision-making process. Ill-structured decisions are those that remain incompletely specified and are ultimately dependent on human judgment. The basis for making those judgments rest on tacit understandings that are never fully explicated.

Recently there has been increased attention on the development of decision support systems. These systems use database, graphics, telecommunications, and simulation models to help managers make semistructured decisions where neither pure procedure, nor pure judgment prevail. The emphasis is on supporting judgment by supplementing the managers decision process with computer power in a way that is understandable and controllable by them.

So far we have introduced the notion of a system with its nested set of input, process and output relations, and we have surveyed the process of management decision-making. Now, we add the perspective of the organization as a system. For this we use the systems approach of C. West Churchman.[1] We understand organizations with a systems approach when we think of the organization with five basic considerations. They are: (1) the resources of the system; (2) the environment of the system; (3) the components of the systems; (4) the objective of the system; and (5) the management of the system.

Resources are everything the system can draw you in carrying out its activities. This includes everything from cash and fixed assets to dependable procedures, to employee morale and client goodwill. Managers often overlook potential resources and fail to take full advantage of their possibilities.

The *environment* includes everything that is outside the system—and thereby outside of its control—that impacts the performance of the system. For the systems approach, defining the environment correctly and adapting to it successfully is the critical managerial function.

The *components* of the organization are its missions and functional programs; that which its procedures accomplish. These production processes of the organization may coincide with a departmental structure, but usually they will cross departmental lines, and are best conceived of as organization-wide programs rather than activities of isolated subunits.

The *objectives* of the organization are the goals it tends to achieve. These goals are contained in the recognized measures of accomplishment, the criteria used for performance evaluation, and the organization's definition of purpose. One must be careful to distinguish the "real" from the merely espoused objectives, and to observe how the organization actually performs when characterizing its operating objectives.

The *management* of the organization is the responsible action taken by its decision-makers. Here we emphasize the manager's involvement in planning and control decisions. Planning decisions set standards, goals and criteria over a future time horizon, and control is a process of comparing actual achievements with planned outcomes and taking corrective action as needed. This is a cybernetic feedback control process in which a standard of performance is established, and results are compared to the standard, prompting a managerical response when necessary.

Application of the Systems View to Libraries

This section presents some images of the way the systems approach can be used to observe and understand the purposeful activity of organizations. The nested cyclic, input/output transformations that characterize the systems approach, as well as the cybernetic control process, lend themselves well to the use of visual imagery.

The intent is that these visual images be used by the manager or systems analyst as a basis for exploring the set of relationships that constitutes the system, as well as a basis for generating other images and emphasizing other relationships. In any event, the images are convenient ways of organizing the systems concepts identified above, and applying them to a library setting.

Figure 5 presents a visual depiction of Churchman's systems approach. It emphasizes the organization's relationship with critical factors in the environment and the demand those relationships put on the system. As elements are changed, the relationships that are emphasized are changed. Also, any feature of the diagram (resources, access, acquisitions) can be further elaborated for detailed exploration. For instance, the management planning and control process can be expanded as indicated in figure 6.

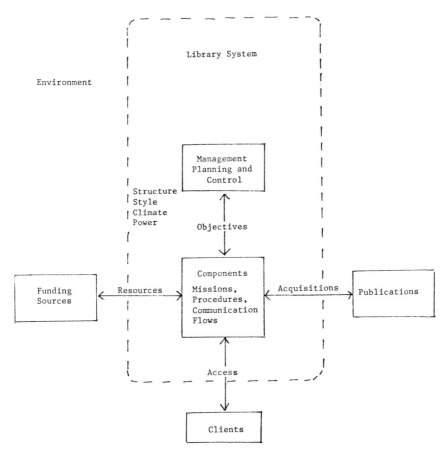

Fig. 5. Diagram of Churchman's Systems Approach

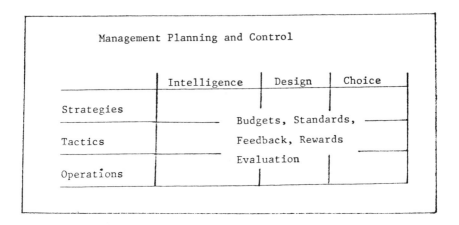

Fig. 6. Management Planning and Control Process

At any level of detail that we wish to expand the diagram, we should not only be concerned with identifying the missing details, but with assessing the overall balance of the system, and using that assessment as a basis for setting priorities. Focusing on one environmental relation while ignoring others, or emphasizing one aspect of the decision-making process over others is usually self-defeating.

The systems view also emphasizes the cyclic character of organizational processes. Figure 7 is a depiction of the library as a two-cycle system of serving clients and building a collection interacting with an environment of knowledge creation and of publications. This basic model can also be expanded, as in figure 8, to reveal subsystems in each cycle and their interrelations. The process of expansion and exploration can continue as each subsystem itself is depicted as a cycle of interrelated activities. Once again, the benefit of this type of analysis is to assist in identifying critical activities and their interrelationships, unnecessary redundancy, weakness, or overemphasis. In short, it helps to explore the question of balance among the many competing demands placed on the organization.

The final image presented in this section is that of a cybernetic control process. For each activity in the system-in-environment diagram or in the system-cycles diagrams, a control process is implied. The basic elements of that control process are shown in figure 9. The model starts with the familiar input-process-output diagram. Added to it is a monitor that measures system outputs. The outputs are then compared to a standard, goal or norm. Here the standard is shown as the prediction from a model of desired system functioning. If the comparison reveals a difference, an error message is received by the manager, who activates a change in the system, the inputs or the standard.

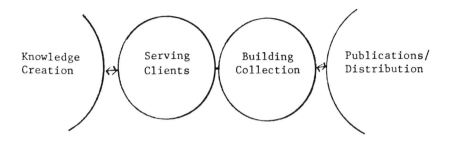

Fig. 7. Representation of the Library as a Two-cycle System

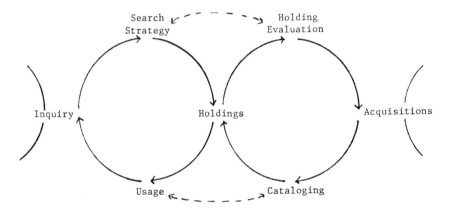

Fig. 8. The Subsystem within the Basic Two-cycle System

The word cybernetic literally means "steersman" and refers to the fact that communication processes set in motion by the output of an activity stimulate corrective responses that tend to bring the outputs back in control. Thus, the system is brought into control by the act of going out of control, and is an error-driven control process.

The cybernetic control model helps us explore the existence or adequacy of the measures of system output, the feedback communication channels, the model of desired system functioning, and the ability of a decision-maker to take corrective action in a time frame that allows the system to remain stable. If the response is too fast or too slow, the system will display oscillations around the standard, but will not converge on it.

We generally recognize three orders of cybernetic feedback control. First order feedback returns system outputs to an acceptable range, given a standard goal. Second order feedback modifies the goal itself to maintain

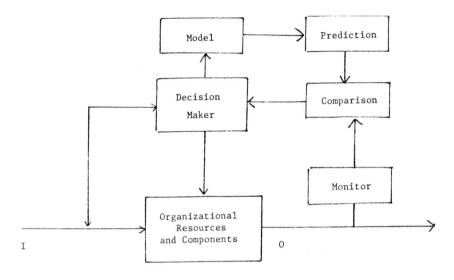

Fig. 9. Diagram of the Basic Elements in the Control Process

an overall strategy in a changing environment, and third order feedback modifies the strategy and purpose of a system based on a learning process that questions the nature of the systems relation with its environment.

Implications for Deriving Management Information from Automation

We now add to the discussion above some further considerations in designing management information systems.

The organization itself—the way it is structured with routine procedures and reporting relations—is a source of management information. These in-place procedures not only provide the positive or negative feedback that enables cybernetic control, they also define the organization's ability to sense changes in the environment, react to disturbances, handle exceptions, implement plans, achieve consensus, and revise plans. The structure and process of the organization thus deserves as much attention as the data processing support available to a particular manager.

Another consideration is that the data system must fit the organization. The style, climate and power that characterizes the management of an organization is critical to effective information system design. Is the structure based on type of client served, library function, geographic location, or a matrix combination? Is the structure centralized or decentralized, formal or informal? Is there agreement on goals? How are unit heads held accountable? What kinds of reward and status systems are in place? How freely does formal and informal communication occur? What style of leadership does the organization display—rational persuasion, inspiration or empathy? How are these tied to the methods of motivating employees? What degree of formality, concern for the privileges of office, responsibility for worker security, and participation in decision-making characterize the organization? Where does power rest in the organization? How is it displayed and used? All these considerations are important because they contribute to the crucial difference between data and information. The data from an automated system will only be informative in an organizational context. To realize its potential value, data must lead to understanding and effective action, both of which are constrained by the organization structure.

We observe that most organizations have a limited number of critical factors that spell the difference between success and mere survival for an organization. This limited number of critical factors follows from the organization's strategic relations with its environment. Key decisions related to these critical factors is where the effort of management information support should be directed. There is practically no limit to the number of decisions and management activities that could be identified and supported with automation. Most of them are not worth the effort. The value of system development is maximized when those key decisions that affect the critical success factors receive the focus of attention and effort.

Another consideration is that a cybernetic control image emphasizes the importance of standards of evaluation and models of system performance. Unless there are standards to which actual outcomes are compared, there can be no stimulus for corrective action. Unless there is at least an implicit model of how the organization should be functioning and how decisions should be made, there is no basis for learning. The definition of standards for evaluation and the identification of the decision models managers do or should use is perhaps the most significant outcome of developing a management information system.

Data to provide management information may be generated from:

1. Reports from operations and transaction-based systems. The reports can be regularly scheduled, ad hoc, or exception based, with content tied to the level and type of decision being supported.
2. Access to database systems, both internal and external, that allow inquiry and special reports.
3. Modeling facilities that allow simulations, statistical analyses and forecasts.

In addition to database access and statistical and graphic analysis, management terminals can also offer time management, project management, message management, and teleconferencing services.

The types of decision support models that can be developed include:

1. probabilistic decision models, where the alternatives and payoffs identified by the decision-maker are combined with their expectations of the occurrence of future events;
2. deterministic simulations showing how a closed-system set of relationships behave over time. Cash flow and budget projections are classic examples of these simulations, and are the basis of financial planning and control;
3. forecasting models where historical experience of demand, usage, etc. is extrapolated to generate data for capacity planning and other purposes; and
4. optimizing models, such as linear programming, where a set of constraints are taken into account in maximizing an objective function.

Perhaps the most common type of managerial support, however, is provided by a set of search, sort and statistical programs tied to a large file representing a portfolio of objects for which the manager has responsibility. For instance, we have recently been involved in developing an acquisition support system for a media center. It consists of a file of potential acquisitions along with a boolean search procedure, sort and statistical procedures, and a report generator. In the development of the system, there were many critical technical issues that needed careful attention and which, in some instances, constrained the design. Yet, the most crucial issues in design centered on how the system was going to change the location of decision-making on acquisitions, with some people losing power and others gaining it.

Although the software of this system is powerful and flexible, its effectiveness will depend on the quality with which managers rank target areas and rate potential acquisitions. This kind of formal quantification is a new behavior that must be learned. Finally, the boolean search procedures are only as good as the questions the decision-makers will ask. The system only presents a potential, and the manager alone has the possibility to realize it which leads to the final implication.

The major reason for the failure of management support systems are organizational—not technical or economic. To be a success, the system must be implemented and used. This is a question of organizational acceptance and individual learning on the part of managers. There is no clear recipe for implementation success, but some prominent features of systems that succeed are:

1. that there is a strong felt need on the part of managers to develop the system;
2. that top administration personnel supports and fosters the effort;

3. that all affected parties are actively, meaningfully involved in the development; and
4. the system is congruent with the climate, style and power of the organization.

The System Development Process

This section gives a brief overview of an ideal system development process. The design, installation and evaluation of management support systems is a tightly woven cycle that displays an evolutionary, adaptive learning capacity. It is an iterative, recursive process that is easily separated into neat stages only in papers such as this. Figure 10 depicts the system development process as beginning with a system plan. My intention is to highlight the need to identify the critical decisions needing support based on the organization's strategic relations with its environment. The issues of efficiency versus effectiveness discussed in section one must be resolved in the planning process with a time-phased identification of priorities. The plan should chart the organization's forward movement by maintaining a balance among its key functions, and its level of managerial and technical sophistication.

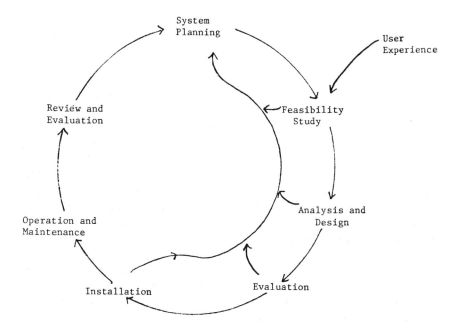

Fig. 10. Diagram of the System Development Process

The planning process, combined with the experience of user groups, creates a felt need for change and system development. It is this felt need for change which should drive system design. The feasibility study is an opportunity to assess the quality of this need and to test the economic, technical and operational validity of the proposed development. It is important here to focus on the decisions that will be supported, their significance and the impact the system will have on them. This requires that the study team understand the decision process in question, and that they do not merely assume that automation will enhance it.

The proposal should be assessed in terms of its fit with the style, climate and power of the organization and with the openness of the parties involved to accept a change. This requires that there be a dissatisfaction with the existing state of affairs and a willingness to experiment and learn new behaviors as a group, as well as at an individual level.

Analysis and design requires active involvement and support between the manager and the system analyst or technical experts. The best form of this involvement combines a sharing of design responsibility with a sense of mutual understanding, in which each participant respects and attempts to understand the perspective and concerns of the other. This type of involvement requires a significant time commitment by managers, and if they are not prepared to give it, perhaps the felt need is not as great as was at first thought.

The analysis and design stage can follow a top-down or a bottom-up progression. Top-down entails movement from goals and objectives to a logical system that meets their requirements, while bottom-up entails starting with existing procedures and processes and designing an improved system. Usually both used in conjunction with each other will prove most effective. This is because the decision process is not just a rational process of selecting best courses of action.

As mentioned above, the procedures, programs, offices, and routines are an important, organizationally-embedded source of decision-making and action. In fact, I would argue that most organizational decisions are determined by the interaction of routine organizational procedures. The decision process is also a political, disjointed one in which coalitions form and dissolve as threats and opportunities change. Any analysis that emphasizes the purely rational at the expense of appreciating the procedural and political is risking implementation failure.

An evaluation of the design should be performed before programming and testing. The risk of implementation failure should be reassessed, as well as the value of the system to the intended decisions. Designs have a way of being modified over time and this provides a test that the expected impact on crucial decisions has not been lost.

KEN DOWLIN
Director
Pikes Peak Library District

LYNN MAGRATH
Associate Director
Pikes Peak Library District

Beyond the Numbers—
A Decision Support System

The degree of sophistication of an organization's information system is indicated by its placement in the stages of evolution of general information systems. The first stage is the automation of clerical tasks. The second stage is redesign of the system and subsystem integration. The third stage is support for middle management decisions, and the fourth stage is support for top level, decision-making.[1] The library community has progressed through the stage of automating clerical functions. There are computerized systems for almost all such systems in libraries. These systems are not in operation in every library, nor are all of the systems in operation in any single library—but the pieces are there. Libraries are just starting into the second stage—systems redesign and integration. There are a handful of libraries that have implemented major portions of an integrated system. There are even fewer libraries that have reached the third stage and almost no library that has reached the fourth stage.

The Pikes Peak Library District (PPLD) completed the first stage in the development of its general information system in 1979, the majority of the second and third stages at this writing, and has embarked on a serious effort to complete the fourth stage.

Information for top level decision-making must, by necessity, include data from sources that cannot be automated. It is very difficult to include information about the environment on the library's computer in a way that the computer can collect that data in a routine fashion. The process of coping with changes in the external environment may be the most difficult part of the planning process, and may be the most crucial.[2] All of the routine data about the operations of the organization which are automated may be collected and stored by the computer. The computer may even organize the data in a way to assist its interpretation. And though the computer allows us to collect a large mass of data easily, the task that remains is to design the systems that provide the framework for this data, the analysis of the data, and the criteria which the computer may use to identify exceptions.

While designing the computer system is an important component of the decision support system (DSS), a recent study by Cheney and Dickson supports the proposition "that it doesn't make a great deal of difference what computer technology an organization employs....The important thing is how it is used." The results of their study, published in *Academy of Management Journal*, indicated (1) how user interaction takes place, (2) how employees are managed, and (3) how computer resources are allocated within the organization. All are more important in terms of user satisfaction and use of the system than what hardware or software is employed.[3]

Robert N. Anthony provides a useful framework for categorizing the collected data into levels. He suggests that the information be assigned to three classes: (1) strategic planning, (2) management control, and (3) operational control. Strategic planning is defined as the process of deciding on objectives of the organization, on changes in these objectives, on the resources used to attain these objectives, and on the policies that are to govern the acquisition, use and disposition of these resources. In the public library, strategic planning is the responsibility of the board of trustees, where thay have the legal authority to do so. If not, it is the responsibility of the city or county council, or other elected body. The library director is also involved in providing recommendations to the board for their consideration. In academic or school libraries, strategic planning is done by the entity charged with the overall responsibility for the institution, and the library is usually considered an entity for the implementing of total organization goals.

Management control is the process by which managers ensure that resources are obtained and used effectively and efficiently in the accomplishment of the organization's objectives. In the library world, this is usually the task of the library administration.

Operational control is the process of assuring that specific tasks are carried out effectively and efficiently. This level is the responsibility of the department or division supervisors.[4]

A DSS is not a single invention or method. It is a new direction or philosophy in computer-supported management.[5] It builds a database to answer some question or to work on a problem as yet undefined or unstructured.[6] Such a system also provides the ability to manipulate the data to answer those questions that have not been formulated at the time that the system is designed. The payoff for a DSS is its ability to extend the range and capability of managers to make decisions without imposing solutions.[7]

"The old MIS [management information system] design approach begins with existing systems, and produces benefits by chance. The approach that [should be followed] focuses on key tasks and decisions leading to more effective decisions, and then attacks the problem of designing information systems to support those tasks."[8] The following general model may be adopted as a guideline for a DSS adaptable to the library setting. This model holds that:

1. Data categories should be mutually exclusive.
2. Data should be capable of aggregation.
3. Data should be capable of disaggregation to very specific levels.
4. The data systems should accommodate complex organizations and small organizations equally well.
5. Data categories should be understandable by the parent organization and lay persons, as well as librarians and library staff.
6. Data should be organized into a framework intelligible to both lay and library persons.

The DSS for the Pikes Peak Library is the result of an amalgamation of various factors which include the data that has been historically collected; adding methodologies to aggregate data; designing a framework for the total system; using the report writer on "Maggie" (**PPLD**'s computer) to store, organize, and retrieve the data; adding mathematical formulas that provide indicators for measurement; and including new data that had relevance. It has been in development for over five years, since one of the original objectives of the automation of the library operations was to provide management information. As the automation of the library's functions became reality, significant elements were added to the DSS. A look at the overall scope of "Maggie's Place," the automated environment of the Pikes Peak Library, is contained in Ken Dowlin's book titled *The Promise of the Electronic Library.*[9]

The functions of the DSS are:

1. *To generate the monthly and annual reports required by external entitities (accountability).* Current data generated for these accountability reports is often compared with historical trends and provides support for ongoing decision-making by managers and supervisors. The resulting decisions will directly affect the operation of the library on a short- and medium-range basis. This information can be a valuable tool in making decisions such as which programs should be changed or eliminated. Because many of these same accountability statistics are kept by most libraries they provide a point of comparison between libraries as well as a device for internal comparison and external reporting.

2. *To provide structured data that can be manipulated to provide analysis on a scheduled basis.* "Scheduled analysis" is generally performed

to evaluate a specific function longitudinally. This type of analysis may be carried on indefinitely in order to provide continuous input for assessing the performance of a particular variable. Two examples are, the inventory use ratio (IUR) and the patron use ratio (PUR). These two measures are routinely generated by PPLD's computer in response to specific information needs which were not met by the traditional level one accountability measures. The IUR was created to confirm the validity of the materials selection decisions made by the PPLD librarians. Once a month the IUR reports the percentage of each classification that is checked out at the point of data collection. Longitudinal studies using the inventory use ration will confirm or deny the validity of the assumption that the IUR is an accurate predictor of future use, hence a useful tool for determining future materials selections.

The patron use ratio has provided some surprising information concerning use patterns of patrons. Recent studies show that the majority of library card usage by patrons is primarily from those who have obtained their library cards within the last year. As this indicator has been developed recently, monthly data collection over the next two years will be used to validate the early findings.

3. *To answer a specific question or to validate assumptions (investigation).* Do the members of the community perceive the library as a community information center, as a community communications center, and as a source of books and materials for the community? Does the community perceive the library as an organization which operates efficiently? These are the types of questions which provide valuable input for future decision-making concerning overall library goal setting and resource allocation. The perceptual survey was designed to answer these specific questions. This survey has shown that the library has exceeded its goal when 51 percent of the community perceives the library as a materials center and when 51 percent of the community believes that the library operates efficiently. If the board of directors continues to support these specific goals, this survey will be repeated again in approximately two years to find out if the library has made progress toward the accomplishment of the other two goals.

4. *To provide intersystem validation (validation).* This level affords the decision-maker the option of comparing the data gathered by the specific studies conducted at level three. For example, the perceptual survey contains data detailing how many times the respondents (a representative sample) have used the library within the last year. This information can be used to double check and validate the results found in the patron tenure reports. Information regarding the sex and age of users can also be validated using these two tools.

The initial framework for the DSS was modeled after the proposed framework developed by the National Center for Higher Education Management.[10] Significant changes have occurred since the PPLD system was documented in *Library Effectiveness: A State of the Art* in 1980.[11]

In 1979 the library board of trustees adopted a long-range plan that contained the statement of the mission of the library and its proposed goals.[12] They decided that the mission of the library is (1) to serve as the resource center for published materials for the community, (2) to serve as the community information center, (3) to serve as the community communication center, and (4) to operate as an efficient organization with goal attainment to be planned on a consistent basis.

Goals were adopted which required that 51 percent of the community should perceive the library as meeting the needs of the community for each of the mission elements. In 1980 it was estimated that the library met or exceeded the requirements for a resource center (51 percent or more); that, as an information center, it was below the level of the goal (less than 30 percent); that its communications were below the level of the goal (less than 10 percent); and that its efficiency was around the goal (51 percent).

In 1981, the community was surveyed to determine its perception of the library. The hypotheses of this survey were:

1. That 51 percent of the community perceived the library as a materials resource center for the community (predicted less than 50 percent).
2. That 51 percent of the community perceived the library as an information center for the community (predicted less than 30 percent).
3. That 51 percent of the community perceived the library as a communications center for the community (predicted less than 10 percent).
4. That 51 percent of the community perceived that the library operates in an efficient manner (predicted less than 50 percent).

Methodology

The telephone survey was conducted by students in a graduate level statistics class during fall semester 1981. The respondents were chosen on a random basis from the Colorado Springs metropolitan area telephone book. Only one questionnaire per household was completed, and surveyors were instructed not to interview potential respondents under the age of fourteen. A total of 214 people were questioned. If more than one answer was given to a question the response was left blank by the data coder. Written guidelines were provided to each surveyor including such instructions as a standard definition of *efficient* and other anticipated points of clarification the surveyor might not be automatically familiar with. The questions relating directly to the goals gave the respondent three possible choices: agree, disagree, or don't know.

Characteristics of Respondents

The survey respondents were between the ages of twenty-five and thirty-four years of age (27 percent). The age groups thirty-five to forty-four and forty-five to fifty-four were second in frequency with each category containing 18 percent of the respondents. Of these, 65 percent of the respondents were women.

Total Income of Respondents' Households

Of the respondents surveyed, 28 percent reported their total family income to be between $10,000 to $19,000; 20 percent reported their total family income to be between $20,000 to $29,999; 16 percent reported their total family income to be between $0 to $9,999; and 10 percent reported the total family income to be between $30,000 to $39,999. Demographic data were collected whenever possible in categories corresponding to those used by the U.S. Census to validate the sample. The income percentages do not differ significantly from those reported by the 1980 census for the population sampled. At this writing, age and educational level data are unavailable for the 1980 census of the tracts involved.

Respondents' Use of the Library in the Past Year

The telephone survey also provided information regarding respondents' use of the library in the last year. The survey contained a good representation of both users and nonusers. Of those surveyed, 33 percent used the library zero times in the last year; 30 percent had used the library six times or less; 25 percent had used the library approximately twelve times; 9 percent had used the library approximately fifty-two times; and 3 percent reported use of the library more than fifty-two times in the last year.

Conclusions

Of those surveyed, 67 percent perceived the library as a place to find "materials" (only 2 percent disagreed, the remaining 31 percent didn't know). In addition, 39 percent of those surveyed perceived the library as a place to find information (only 4 percent disagreed, the remaining 57 percent didn't know). Well above the predicted percentile, 34 percent perceived the library as a center for communications for the community (5 percent disagreed, and 61 percent didn't know).

Even more surprising were the efficiency figures: 73 percent perceived the library as using its resources efficiently (4 percent disagreed, and 23 percent stated they did not know). One of the most striking points to note is that so few people disagree in any of the categories, particularly "efficiency." A table of the current DSS is helpful for determining the relationship of the components to Anthony's levels for decision-making (see table 1).

Reports Produced by the Pikes Peak Library District

Compliments and Complaints. These are comments on the library and its operations by the users or nonusers. They are written and sent to the supervisor and manager concerned, the library director, and the board of trustees. The comments are not aggregated, but they do provide a sense of the operation of the library.

Budget and Expenditures. This is a monthly report of all budgeted amounts and expenditures by operational unit and line item. Each supervisor and manager receives the section on his area of responsibility, and an aggregate is provided to the board of trustees and external agencies. This data can be displayed on a terminal at any time with the data current to the minute. A sample report is contained in figure 2.

Revenues. This monthly report indicates the revenue received and compares it to previous time periods. Since the PPLD is a semi-autonomous agency, expenditures cannot exceed revenues. Since the majority of the budget is based on estimates from the county assessor, care must be taken to monitor cash in the event the estimates are not accurate. This data is available online to the financial development office and the director. The revenue report is illustrated in figure 3.

Service Indicators. These totals are provided monthly to the board, director and managers. The data is loaded into the design support system by the division that is collecting them or the computer from operational programs. This report and the historical data can be accessed and analyzed online. Figure 4 provides a sample report. Figure 4a shows the codes and definitions for the items. The items are grouped under the goal to relate to goal attainment.

Inventory Count. This count is a historical continuation of the long standing tradition of counting items added and deleted. A complete inventory of the collection using the computer has just been finished. When this inventory is validated, the figures in the computer will displace those of the manual system. A sample report is contained in figure 5.

TABLE 1
CURRENT DECISION SUPPORT SYSTEMS FOR
PIKES PEAK LIBRARY DISTRICT

Board of Trustees
(strategic planning)

Compliments and complaints   (m)
Budget and expenditure reports   (m)
Revenue reports   (m)
Service indicators reports   (m)
Inventory counts   (m)
Perceptual surveys   (nr)
Project status reports   (m) (nr)

Director
(strategic planning and management control)

Inventory use ratio exceptions   (m) (o)
Inventory use ratios   (m) (o)
Budget and expenditures by department and division   (m) (o)
Flow through expenditures and revenues by account   (m)
Patron use   (m) (o)
Patron tenure   (nr)
Perceptual survey   (nr)
Security reports   (d)
Online catalog use counts   (d) (m)
Compliments and complaints   (d)
Critical incidents   (d)
Item information   (o)
Online catalog survey   (nr)
Project status reports   (m) (nr)
Service indicators reports   (m) (o)
Revenue reports   (m) (o)

Managers
(management control and operations control)

Public Services Department
    Service indicators report   (m) (o)
    Budget and expenditures report   (m) (o)
    Materials encumbrances   (m)
    Inventory use ratio   (m) (o)
    Inventory use ratio exceptions   (m) (o)
    Patron use   (m) (o)
    Information and reference detail report   (m) (o)
    Catalog use counts   (d)
    Compliments and complaints   (d)
    Perceptual survey   (nr)
    Critical incidents   (d)
    Online catalog survey   (nr)
    Periodicals use report   (t)
    Item information   (o)

TABLE 1—*Continued*

Technical Services Department
    Inventory counts (m)
    Critical incidents (m)
    Challenged materials (d)
    Item information (o)
    Material encumbrances (m)
    Budget and expenditure reports (m) (o)

Operations Department
    Service indicators (m) (o)
    Circulation detail report (m)
    Security reports (d)
    Critical incidents (d)
    Patron information (o)
    Item information (o)

Ridefinders (project)
    Service indicators (m) (o)
    Budget and expenditures (m) (o)
    Project status reports (m)

o—Data can be accessed and analyzed online
nr—Data is collected only when required
d—Daily reports
m—Monthly reports
t—Data is collected three times per year

Perceptual Survey. This survey provides information concerning the community's perceptions toward the library in relation to the library's mission. Figure 6 shows the perceptual survey data.

Project Status Reports. These reports are generated by special projects such as the "Past as Prologue Series," funded by the National Endowment for the Humanities, and Ridefinders, which is funded by the Pikes Peak Area Council of Governments and operated by the library.

Inventory Use Ratio Exceptions. This report is created from the inventory use ratio program. After the inventory use ratio is calculated, the program calculates the mean for all the classes, the standard deviation, and identifies the classes that are over one standard deviation above or below the mean. These classes are identified as exceptions allowing investigation into each specific class. A sample report is shown in figure 7.

Inventory Use Ratio. When commanded to do so, the computer reads the entire inventory file and produces the inventory use ratio report. This run is usually done on the last Sunday of each month. The computer counts the number of items in each class, counts the number of items checked out, and the number of items that are noncirculating. The inventory use ratio is calculated by dividing the number of items checked out by

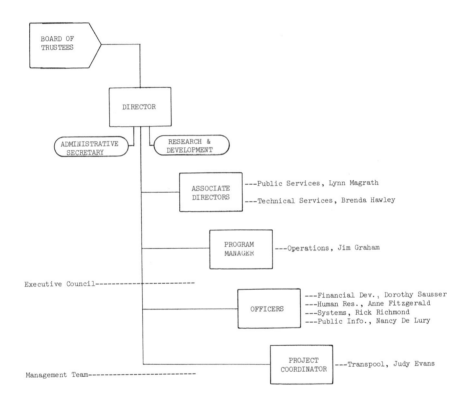

Fig. 1. Organizational Structure of the Pikes Peak Library District (PPLD)

	Budgeted	Expended To Date	Expended This Mo.	Current Balance
SALARIES	$1,237,388.00	$305,974.18	$104,237.88	$ 931,413.82
HOURLY SALARIES	60,862.00	13,782.36	4,439.90	47,079.64
TEMPORARY HOURLY	74,721.00	23,923.33	8,756.94	50,797.67
PARTIAL PAYMENT	8,794.00	877.45	1,742.23	7,916.55
PAYROLL CONTRIBUTIONS	233,777.50	54,570.05	17,105.03	179,207.45
TRAINING	9,270.00	2,426.17	1,397.79	6,843.83
*TOTAL PERSONNEL	$1,624,812.50	$401,553.54	$134,195.31	$1,223.258.96
LEASED BOOKS	$ 63,224.44	$ 6,715.80	$ 1,755.00	$ 56,508.64
BOOKS	128,810.16	15,264.17	9,919.60	113,545.99
MICROFORMS	27,358.90	2,277.65	0.00	25,081.25
SUBSCRIPTIONS	31,483.00	27,890.48	830.41	3,592.52
STANDING ORDERS	24,066.00	2,753.75	1,403.79	21,312.25
PREVIEW MATERIALS	45,460.00	13,782.45	7,176.61	31,677.55
FILMS & FILMSTRIPS	8,350.00	593.09	0.00	7,756.91
BINDING	10,000.00	3,183.46	1,880.87	6,816.54
RECORDINGS	2,150.00	44.80	0.00	2,105.20
FRAMED PRINTS	0.00	0.00	0.00	0.00
*TOTAL MATERIALS	$ 340,902.50	$ 72,505.65	$ 22,966.28	$ 268,396.85
GENERAL SUPPLIES	$ 26,945.00	$ 3,916.05	$ 361.30	$ 23,028.95
SPECIAL SUPPLIES	90,271.63	26,918.14	4,956.55	63,353.49
*TOTAL SUPPLIES	$ 117,216.63	$ 30,834.19	$ 5,317.85	$ 86,382.44
COMPUTER OPERATION	$ 80,412.00	$ 21,397.28	$ 2,294.08	$ 59,014.72
TELEPHONE	32,678.00	7,925.79	2,956.44	24,752.21
UTILITIES	76,641.00	15,448.38	10,217.27	61,192.62
CONTRACT SERVICES	142,422.73	34,829.89	13,627.65	107,592.84
FACILITIES RENTAL	57,675.00	18,526.50	4,681.00	39,148.50
VEHICLE MAINTENANCE	13.040.00	2,690.72	2,361.98	10,349.28
INSURANCE	10,803.00	237.00	237.00	10,566.00
*TOTAL FACILITIES	$ 413,671.73	$101,055,56	$ 36,375.42	$ 312,616.17
BUILDING REPAIR	$ 41,200.00	$ 16,757.49	$ 730.77	$ 24,442.51
FURNITURE	3,706.00	609.00	436.50	3,097.00
VEHICLES	4,300.00	0.00	0.00	4,300.00
EQUIPMENT	26,235.72	12,154.40	3,319.99	14,081.32
*TOTAL CAPITAL ITEMS	$ 75,441.72	$ 29,520.89	$ 4,487.26	$ 45,920.83
INSTITUTIONAL DUES	$ 2,100.00	$ 1,085.00	$ 0.00	$ 1,015.00
TREAS./AUDITOR FEES	33,000.00	4,740.09	3,822.04	28,259.91
RESEARCH & DEVELOPMENT	170,286.00	4,223.27	1,023.41	166,062.73
MILEAGE & TRAVEL	12,511.00	1,921.37	435.50	10.589.63
*TOTAL MISCELLANEOUS	$ 217,897.00	$ 11,969.73	$ 4,409.95	$ 205,927.27
*** TOTAL BUDGET ***	$2,789,942.08	$647,439.56	$207,752.07	$2,142.502.52

Fig. 2. Sample Budget Report for the PPLD

MARCH, 1982

Revenues

	This Month	Year-To-Date	Last Year This Month	% Collected	Estimated
Property tax	251,470.85	449,586.43	244,277.18	21.4%	2,100,374.00
Delinquent Tax & Int.	1,178.39	7,563.68		59.2%	12,775.00
Auto Tax	13,438.23	56,628.86	14,872.22	33.3%	170,000.00
Miscellaneous	4,336.04	11,650.60	2,827.93	33.2%	35,000.00
Interest		250.78		1.2%	20,000.00
Flow thru	18,980.82	66,413.27	26,697.88	17.3%	381,821.00
General Fund	270,423.51	525,680.35	261,977.33	22.4%	2,338,122.00
TOTAL	289,404.33	592,093.62	288,675.21	21.7%	2,719,943.00

Expenditures

	This Month	Year-To-Date	Last Year This Month	% Expended	Estimated
General Fund	186,093.48	584,012.02	232,411.68	24%	2,408,121.68
Flow thru	21,658.59	63,427.54	20,978.15	17%	381,820.40
TOTAL	207,752.07	647,439.56	253,389.83	23%	2,789,942.08

Fig. 3. Sample Revenue Report for the PPLD

STATISTICS REPORT
March, 1982

GOAL: COMMUNICATIONS

Goal	Function	This Month	YTD	LYTD	% Difference
C	CALLS	15112	42996	36996	+16%
C	ILT	544	1251	601	+33%
C	LDB	1771	5844	7915	−26%
C	NLDB	24	59	64	−08%
C	OUTSIDE	22	57	49	+16%
C	P OUT/S	1215	2216	783	+183%

Networking

Goal	Function	This Month	YTD	LYTD	% Difference
C	HANDLED	580	1703	1609	+06%
C	LOANED	542	1361	626	+117%
C	BORROWED	142	456	293	+56%

GOAL: INFORMATION

Services

Goal	Function	This Month	YTD	LYTD	% Difference
I	PROGRAMS	111	229	305	−33%
I	P PROGS	4186	8801	11298	−22%
I	QA-D	7927	19567	23172	−16%
I	TOURS	18	57	25	+128%
I	P TOURS	406	1292	354	+265%

RideFinders

Goal	Function	This Month	YTD	LYTD	% Difference
I	# CALLS	391	1189	1278	−07%
I	# MATCH	212	397	312	+27%
I	# ADDED	111	391	739	−47%

GOAL: RESOURCE

Services

Goal	Function	This Month	YTD	LYTD	% Difference
R	CIRC	100655	266886	279019	−04%
R	QA-S	23020	57083	63619	−10%
R	REC BOR	2425	6870	6203	+11%
R	RSERVES	886	4324	7032	−39%
R	USE	60241	153664	161572	−05%

Fig. 4. Sample Service Indicator Report for the PPLD

CALLS - telephone calls received

ILT - intra library transfers, books being transferred from branches or main within the district.

LDB - library's data base, data base search made of library information.

NLDB - non-library data base, data base searches of other than the library's.

OUTSIDE - presentations the staff make outside of the library.

P OUT/S - number of people at presentations outside of the library.

PROGRAMS - presentations by the staff presented in the library.

P PROGS - number of people at presentations presented in the library.

TOURS - number of library tours given.

P TOURS - number of people given tours.

QA-D - questions answered-directory, questions answered for patrons which does not require any kind of searching in materials (i.e. where are the 900's?)

CIRC - circulation, number of books checked out

QA-S - questions answered-search, questions asked by patrons requiring searching for the answer.

REC BOR - reciprocal borrowing, number of items checked out within the district by patrons who do not belong to the district but belong to the Plains and Peaks Regional Library System.

RSERVES - number of items placed on reserve.

USE - number of people who come in the door.

RideFinders: # CALLS - number of telephone calls received.

ADDED - number of people inserted in the computer for matching.

MATCH - number of people matched to share rides.

Fig. 4a. Codes for the Service Indicator Report

March, 1982

INVENTORY	TOTAL MONTHLY		TOTAL INVENTORY	THIS YEAR TO DATE		LAST YEAR TO DATE	
	+	−		+	−	+	−
Books (adult & youth)	2,057	748	302,258	5,500	1,865	5,021	2,301
Books (juvenile)	119	421	98,068	2,555	1,633	1,357	1,057
Books (popular)	226	85	14,299	462	334	879	394
Films (8mm)			273				
Films (16mm)			119		1		
Manuscripts			431				
Map Case, Blueprints			2,330				
Maps			769				
Microfiche			5,953				
Negatives (L.H.)							
Pamphlets, CO			265				
Prints, Framed			332		1		
Recordings			5,192		129	105	146
Slides (35mm Color)			312				
Tapes	4 kits		139 (125 k)	16k			
Transparencies			21				
SUBTOTALS	2,434	1,254	430,761	8,566	3,963	7,485	3,898
Microfilm Reels			5,517				
Vertical File	776	38	34,742	1,592	2,346	2,559	2,898
Pictures	166	108	37,035	274	127	273	91
Vertical File Music			2,042				
Curiosities			51				
TOTALS	3,376	1,400	510,148	10,432	6,436	10,317	6,887
OTHER ITEMS OF INTEREST THAT ARE PROCESSED							
Gift Books	406			880		694	
Gift Records						7	31
Bindery Books	302			618			
Priorities	381			1,317			
Government Documents	45			52		123	
Leased Books	361	573		1,458	1,535		
Periodicals	910						
Mending Books	219			241			

Fig. 5. Sample Inventory Count Report for the PPLD

COMPONENT	ESTIMATE	GOAL	AGREE	DISAGREE	DON'T KNOW
Materials	50%	51%	67%	2%	31%
Information	30%	51%	39%	4%	57%
Communications	10%	51%	34%	5%	61%
Efficiency	50%	51%	73%	4%	23%

Fig. 6. Perceptual Survey Figures for the PPLD

DATE	MEAN	STD	EXCPLUS	EXCMINUS
19-APR-82	0.118782	0.094133	000	
19-APR-82	0.118782	0.094133		010
19-APR-82	0.118782	0.094133		040
19-APR-82	0.118782	0.094133		060
19-APR-82	0.118782	0.094133		310
19-APR-82	0.118782	0.094133	510	
19-APR-82	0.118782	0.094133	560	
19-APR-82	0.118782	0.094133	650	
19-APR-82	0.118782	0.094133	690	
19-APR-82	0.118782	0.094133	770	
19-APR-82	0.118782	0.094133		C
19-APR-82	0.118782	0.094133	E	
19-APR-82	0.118782	0.094133		G
19-APR-82	0.118782	0.094133	H	
19-APR-82	0.118782	0.094133		I
19-APR-82	0.118782	0.094133	L	
19-APR-82	0.118782	0.094133	N	
19-APR-82	0.118782	0.094133	P	
19-APR-82	0.118782	0.094133	Q	
19-APR-82	0.118782	0.094133		R
19-APR-82	0.118782	0.094133	S	
19-APR-82	0.118782	0.094133		T
19-APR-82	0.118782	0.094133	X	
19-APR-82	0.118782	0.094133	Y	
19-APR-82	0.118782	0.094133	Z	
19-APR-82	0.118782	0.094133		

Fig. 7. Sample Inventory Use Ratio Exceptions Report for the PPLD

the number of items in the class. The heading OT (see fig. 8) indicates this number. The OTR heading in figure 8 is the inventory use ratio adjusted for noncirculating items. The results are stored in a datatrieve (the report writer provided by Digital Equipment Corporation) file, from which the report is printed. Records in this file can be retrieved by an element, sorted, formatted for printing, and printed. The results can be arranged by any of the elements. The ability to access this file, as well as the other elements in the DSS via the terminal, allows messaging of the data and the output. Figure 8 shows a report of the inventory use ratio. This program has added a new dimension to our ability to analyze collection usage. It is, perhaps, the best collection planning tool available. It has been used to test the ability of the librarians in information services and reference to estimate the materials needed for the public. Their predictions as to the use of the different classes correlated with the inventory use ratio 80 percent of the time. A ratio for each class can be displayed or printed which allows the trends to be discerned (see fig. 8a). Figure 8b shows the inventory use ratio for new books, and figure 8c shows the inventory use ratio for the 590s.

Flow Through Expenditures. This report shows the revenues and expenditures for all nongeneral funds. The expenditures in these programs are directly tied to the sources of the funds, and it is important that expenditures do not occur prior to receipt of funds. Examples are grants, federal employment programs, donations and programs that must recover their cost.

Patron Use. This program checks the date of last use for each patron record and tallies them by class. The classes are less than 30 days, 60 days, 180 days, one year, two years, three years, four years, and five years. A report is shown in figure 9. This program is run on demand.

Patron Tenure. This program compares the date the patron received his card with its most recent use. The results indicate the number of current users who received their cards within ninety days, one year, two years, three years, four years, and five years. The results are shown in figure 10. This program is run on demand.

Security Reports. These reports are daily logs of unusual occurrences in the library. They include the number of patrons trapped by the book security system and other security disturbances.

Online Catalog Use Count. This is a command log by type and terminal for activity on the online catalog and inventory system. It is printed out daily and accumulated monthly. Since the online catalog is new, this program was established to provide data on its use. A sample of the program is in figure 11.

DATE	TYPE	CLASS	TTL	OUT	REF	OT	OTR	SUM
19-Apr-82	DEWEY	040	4	0	1	0.0000	0.0000	0.0000
19-Apr-82	DEWEY	060	92	0	44	0.0000	0.0000	0.0000
19-Apr-82	SHELF	T	16	0	0	0.0000	0.0000	0.0000
19-Apr-82	SHELF		0	0	0	0.0000	0.0000	0.0000
19-Apr-82	SHELF	G	2,952	5	0	0.0017	0.0000	0.0000
19-Apr-82	SHELF	C	11,162	20	0	0.0018	0.0000	0.0000
19-Apr-82	SHELF	R	13,827	42	0	0.0030	0.0000	0.0000
19-Apr-82	DEWEY	310	1,141	9	998	0.0079	0.0629	0.0000
19-Apr-82	SHELF	I	173	2	0	0.0116	0.0000	0.0000
19-Apr-82	DEWEY	010	1,372	16	1,042	0.0117	0.0485	0.0000
19-Apr-82	DEWEY	050	238	6	192	0.0252	0.1304	0.0000
19-Apr-82	SHELF	B	3,505	89	0	0.0254	0.0000	0.0000
19-Apr-82	DEWEY	860	598	18	5	0.0301	0.0304	0.0000
19-Apr-82	SHELF	K	63	2	0	0.0317	0.0000	0.0000
19-Apr-82	DEWEY	840	785	25	13	0.0318	0.0324	0.0000
19-Apr-82	DEWEY	960	297	10	3	0.0337	0.0340	0.0000
19-Apr-82	DEWEY	320	3,678	125	438	0.0340	0.0386	0.0000
19-Apr-82	DEWEY	090	53	2	7	0.0377	0.0435	0.0000
19-Apr-82	DEWEY	850	226	9	3	0.0398	0.0404	0.0000
19-Apr-82	DEWEY	920	14,211	617	2,729	0.0434	0.0537	0.0000
19-Apr-82	DEWEY	080	85	4	4	0.0471	0.0494	0.0000
19-Apr-82	DEWEY	500	1,610	78	520	0.0484	0.0716	0.0000
19-Apr-82	DEWEY	400	101	5	1	0.0495	0.0500	0.0000
19-Apr-82	DEWEY	030	1,427	75	925	0.0526	0.1494	0.0000
19-Apr-82	DEWEY	880	239	13	4	0.0544	0.0553	0.0000
19-Apr-82	DEWEY	870	107	6	2	0.0561	0.0571	0.0000
19-Apr-82	DEWEY	380	3,131	177	1,107	0.0565	0.0875	0.0000
19-Apr-82	DEWEY	820	4,364	249	314	0.0571	0.0615	0.0000
19-Apr-82	DEWEY	830	769	44	24	0.0572	0.0591	0.0000
19-Apr-82	DEWEY	890	731	42	19	0.0575	0.0590	0.0000
19-Apr-82	DEWEY	550	3,018	174	1,299	0.0577	0.1012	0.0000
19-Apr-82	DEWEY	570	2,320	136	356	0.0586	0.0692	0.0000
19-Apr-82	DEWEY	980	253	15	3	0.0593	0.0600	0.0000
19-Apr-82	DEWEY	340	3,356	200	1,087	0.0596	0.0881	0.0000
19-Apr-82	SHELF	V	50	3	0	0.0600	0.0000	0.0000
19-Apr-82	DEWEY	900	1,148	69	162	0.0601	0.0700	0.0000
19-Apr-82	SHELF	A	16	1	0	0.0625	0.0000	0.0000
19-Apr-82	DEWEY	020	1,709	108	556	0.0632	0.0937	0.0000
19-Apr-82	DEWEY	260	522	33	61	0.0632	0.0716	0.0000
19-Apr-82	DEWEY	270	330	21	43	0.0636	0.0732	0.0000
19-Apr-82	DEWEY	970	13,368	857	2,635	0.0641	0.0798	0.0000
19-Apr-82	DEWEY	350	4,400	289	1,176	0.0657	0.0896	0.0000
19-Apr-82	DEWEY	190	446	30	6	0.0673	0.0682	0.0000
19-Apr-82	DEWEY	660	515	35	56	0.0680	0.0763	0.0000
19-Apr-82	DEWEY	540	829	57	175	0.0688	0.0872	0.0000
19-Apr-82	DEWEY	700	1,831	128	192	0.0699	0.0781	0.0000
19-Apr-82	DEWEY	710	655	46	266	0.0702	0.1183	0.0000
19-Apr-82	DEWEY	990	128	9	0	0.0703	0.0703	0.0000
19-Apr-82	DEWEY	810	7,921	560	560	0.0707	0.0761	0.0000

Fig. 8. Sample Inventory Use Ratio Report for the PPLD

DATE	TYPE	CLASS	TTL	OUT	REF	OT	OTR	SUM
19-Apr-82	SHELF		0	0	0	0.0000	0.0000	0.0000
19-Apr-82	DEWEY	000	1,004	233	38	0.2321	0.2412	0.0000
19-Apr-82	DEWEY	010	1,372	16	1,042	0.0117	0.0485	0.0000
19-Apr-82	DEWEY	020	1,709	108	556	0.0632	0.0937	0.0000
19-Apr-82	DEWEY	030	1,427	75	925	0.0526	0.1494	0.0000
19-Apr-82	DEWEY	040	4	0	1	0.0000	0.0000	0.0000
19-Apr-82	DEWEY	050	238	6	192	0.0252	0.1304	0.0000
19-Apr-82	DEWEY	060	92	0	44	0.0000	0.0000	0.0000
19-Apr-82	DEWEY	070	613	44	173	0.0718	0.1000	0.0000
19-Apr-82	DEWEY	080	85	4	4	0.0471	0.0494	0.0000
19-Apr-82	DEWEY	090	53	2	7	0.0377	0.0435	0.0000
19-Apr-82	DEWEY	100	157	23	17	0.1465	0.1643	0.0000
19-Apr-82	DEWEY	110	127	13	6	0.1024	0.1074	0.0000
19-Apr-82	DEWEY	120	253	23	1	0.0909	0.0913	0.0000
19-Apr-82	DEWEY	130	2,296	471	23	0.2051	0.2072	0.0000
19-Apr-82	DEWEY	140	116	9	0	0.0776	0.0776	0.0000
19-Apr-82	DEWEY	150	2,401	490	14	0.2041	0.2053	0.0000
19-Apr-82	DEWEY	160	58	9	1	0.1552	0.1579	0.0000
19-Apr-82	DEWEY	170	518	64	23	0.1236	0.1293	0.0000
19-Apr-82	DEWEY	180	330	42	1	0.1273	0.1277	0.0000
19-Apr-82	DEWEY	190	446	30	6	0.0673	0.0682	0.0000
19-Apr-82	DEWEY	200	381	41	59	0.1076	0.1273	0.0000
19-Apr-82	DEWEY	210	133	14	7	0.1053	0.1111	0.0000
19-Apr-82	DEWEY	220	1,147	128	69	0.1116	0.1187	0.0000
19-Apr-82	DEWEY	230	787	75	64	0.0953	0.1037	0.0000
19-Apr-82	DEWEY	240	991	145	41	0.1463	0.1526	0.0000
19-Apr-82	DEWEY	250	209	17	19	0.0813	0.0895	0.0000
19-Apr-82	DEWEY	260	522	33	61	0.0632	0.0716	0.0000
19-Apr-82	DEWEY	270	330	21	43	0.0636	0.0732	0.0000
19-Apr-82	DEWEY	280	646	66	126	0.1022	0.1269	0.0000
19-Apr-82	DEWEY	290	1,527	178	94	0.1166	0.1242	0.0000
19-Apr-82	DEWEY	300	5,474	504	525	0.0921	0.1018	0.0000
19-Apr-82	DEWEY	310	1,141	9	998	0.0079	0.0629	0.0000
19-Apr-82	DEWEY	320	3,678	125	438	0.0340	0.0386	0.0000
19-Apr-82	DEWEY	330	5,691	551	1,216	0.0968	0.1231	0.0000
19-Apr-82	DEWEY	340	3,356	200	1,087	0.0596	0.0881	0.0000
19-Apr-82	DEWEY	350	4,400	289	1,176	0.0657	0.0896	0.0000
19-Apr-82	DEWEY	360	5,252	507	1,171	0.0965	0.1242	0.0000
19-Apr-82	DEWEY	370	4,122	446	838	0.1082	0.1358	0.0000
19-Apr-82	DEWEY	380	3,131	177	1,107	0.0565	0.0875	0.0000
19-Apr-82	DEWEY	390	7,327	524	353	0.0715	0.0751	0.0000
19-Apr-82	DEWEY	400	101	5	1	0.0495	0.0500	0.0000
19-Apr-82	DEWEY	410	207	33	6	0.1594	0.1642	0.0000
19-Apr-82	DEWEY	420	874	104	163	0.1190	0.1463	0.0000
19-Apr-82	DEWEY	430	123	19	18	0.1545	0.1810	0.0000
19-Apr-82	DEWEY	440	128	21	7	0.1641	0.1736	0.0000
19-Apr-82	DEWEY	450	27	5	3	0.1852	0.2083	0.0000
19-Apr-82	DEWEY	460	262	43	17	0.1641	0.1755	0.0000
19-Apr-82	DEWEY	470	21	3	3	0.1429	0.1667	0.0000

Fig. 8a. Sample Inventory Use Ratio by Class Report for the PPLD

DATE	TYPE	CLASS	TTL	OUT	REF	OT	OTR	SUM
29-Feb-80	SHELF	N	2,008	1,262	0	0.6285	0.0000	0.0000
04-Apr-80	SHELF	N	2,455	1,435	0	0.5845	0.0000	0.0000
05-May-80	SHELF	N	2,097	1,253	0	0.5975	0.0000	0.0000
31-May-80	SHELF	N	3,072	1,833	0	0.5967	0.0000	0.0000
01-Jul-80	SHELF	N	3,473	2,153	0	0.6199	0.0000	0.0000
01-Aug-80	SHELF	N	3,554	2,122	0	0.5971	0.0000	0.0000
03-Sep-80	SHELF	N	3,917	2,172	0	0.5545	0.0000	0.0000
05-Oct-80	SHELF	N	4,608	2,764	0	0.5998	0.0000	0.0000
03-Nov-80	SHELF	N	5,384	3,220	0	0.5981	0.0000	0.0000
30-Nov-80	SHELF	N	6,426	3,635	0	0.5657	0.0000	0.0000
01-Jan-81	SHELF	N	7,515	4,102	0	0.5458	0.0000	0.0000
01-Feb-81	SHELF	N	7,920	3,662	0	0.4624	0.0000	0.0000
01-Mar-81	SHELF	N	8,836	4,637	0	0.5248	0.0000	0.0000
05-Apr-81	SHELF	N	9,488	5,099	0	0.5374	0.0000	0.0000
11-May-81	SHELF	N	9,488	5,099	0	0.5374	0.0000	0.0000
01-Jun-81	SHELF	N	10,007	5,185	0	0.5181	0.0000	0.0000
09-Jul-81	SHELF	N	9,969	5,152	0	0.5168	0.0000	0.0000
31-Aug-81	SHELF	N	9,877	4,766	0	0.4825	0.0000	0.0000
15-Feb-82	SHELF	N	10,945	5,619	0	0.5134	0.0000	0.0000
02-Mar-82	SHELF	N	10,944	5,740	0	0.5245	0.0000	0.0000
19-Apr-82	SHELF	N	9,877	4,766	0	0.4825	0.0000	0.0000

Fig. 8b. Sample Inventory Use Ratio Report for New Books for the PPLD

DATE	TYPE	CLASS	TTL	OUT	REF	OT	OTR	SUM
29-Feb-80	DEWEY	590	4,379	658	29	0.1503	0.1513	0.0000
04-Apr-80	DEWEY	590	4,538	817	30	0.1800	0.1812	0.0000
05-May-80	DEWEY	590	4,388	668	29	0.1522	0.1532	0.0000
31-May-80	DEWEY	590	5,115	636	152	0.1243	0.1281	0.0000
01-Jul-80	DEWEY	590	5,184	603	172	0.1163	0.1203	0.0000
01-Aug-80	DEWEY	590	5,249	653	172	0.1244	0.1286	0.0000
03-Sep-80	DEWEY	590	5,298	565	173	0.1066	0.1102	0.0000
05-Oct-80	DEWEY	590	5,394	882	174	0.1635	0.1690	0.0000
03-Nov-80	DEWEY	590	5,498	833	174	0.1515	0.1565	0.0000
30-Nov-80	DEWEY	590	5,534	794	174	0.1435	0.1481	0.0000
01-Jan-81	DEWEY	590	5,632	552	174	0.0980	0.1011	0.0000
01-Feb-81	DEWEY	590	5,685	713	200	0.1254	0.1300	0.0000
01-Mar-81	DEWEY	590	5,716	1,008	201	0.1763	0.1828	0.0000
05-Apr-81	DEWEY	590	5,873	1,134	250	0.1931	0.2017	0.0000
11-May-81	DEWEY	590	5,873	1,134	250	0.1931	0.2017	0.0000
01-Jun-81	DEWEY	590	5,939	820	255	0.1381	0.1443	0.0000
09-Jul-81	DEWEY	590	5,976	829	253	0.1387	0.1449	0.0000
31-Aug-81	DEWEY	590	5,898	674	253	0.1143	0.1194	0.0000
15-Feb-82	DEWEY	590	6,093	924	256	0.1516	0.1583	0.0000
02-Mar-82	DEWEY	590	6,100	926	256	0.1518	0.1585	0.0000
19-Apr-82	DEWEY	590	5,898	674	253	0.1143	0.1194	0.0000

Fig. 8c. Sample Inventory Use Ratio Report for the 590 Class for the PPLD

UDATE	USEX	UDESIG	UCLASS	UTOTAL	UUSE
14-Mar-82	M	B	30	000069	000.0008
14-Mar-82	M	M	30	000023	000.0003
14-Mar-82	M	P	30	002652	000.0291
14-Mar-82	W	B	30	000204	000.0022
14-Mar-82	W	M	30	000077	000.0008
14-Mar-82	W	P	30	003782	000.0415
14-Mar-82	B	B	30	000027	000.0003
14-Mar-82	B	M	30	000019	000.0002
14-Mar-82	B	P	30	000903	000.0099
14-Mar-82	G	B	30	000042	000.0005
14-Mar-82	G	M	30	000017	000.0002
14-Mar-82	G	P	30	001079	000.0118
14-Mar-82	U	B	30	000009	000.0001
14-Mar-82	U	M	30	000005	000.0001
14-Mar-82	U	P	30	000768	000.0084
14-Mar-82	M	B	90	000051	000.0006
14-Mar-82	M	M	90	000020	000.0002
14-Mar-82	M	P	90	002623	000.0288
14-Mar-82	W	B	90	000096	000.0011
14-Mar-82	W	M	90	000040	000.0004
14-Mar-82	W	P	90	003237	000.0355
14-Mar-82	B	B	90	000024	000.0003
14-Mar-82	B	M	90	000019	000.0002
14-Mar-82	B	P	90	000881	000.0097
14-Mar-82	G	B	90	000039	000.0004
14-Mar-82	G	M	90	000024	000.0003
14-Mar-82	G	P	90	000994	000.0109
14-Mar-82	U	B	90	000008	000.0001
14-Mar-82	U	M	90	000002	000.0000
14-Mar-82	U	P	90	000588	000.0064
14-Mar-82	M	B	180	000040	000.0004
14-Mar-82	M	M	180	000012	000.0001
14-Mar-82	M	P	180	002840	000.0311
14-Mar-82	W	B	180	000125	000.0014
14-Mar-82	W	M	180	000044	000.0005
14-Mar-82	W	P	180	003831	000.0420
14-Mar-82	B	B	180	000051	000.0006
14-Mar-82	B	M	180	000025	000.0003
14-Mar-82	B	P	180	000992	000.0109
14-Mar-82	G	B	180	000048	000.0005
14-Mar-82	G	M	180	000030	000.0003
14-Mar-82	G	P	180	001047	000.0115
14-Mar-82	U	B	180	000005	000.0001
14-Mar-82	U	M	180	000001	000.0000
14-Mar-82	U	P	180	000546	000.0060

Fig. 9. Sample Patron Use Report for the PPLD

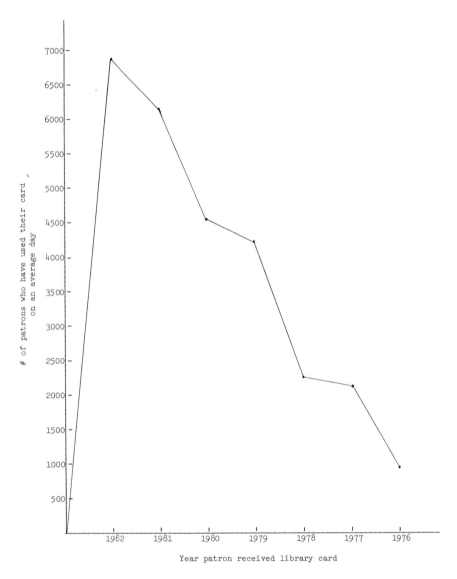

Fig. 10. Graphed Results of the Patron Tenure Report for the PPLD

KEYBOARD		1	2	3	4	5	6	7	8	9	10
KB5:	Cmdr Codie	118	17	15	63	255	18	66	175	727	0.76%
KB6:	Nirvana	6	0	0	0	25	0	0	93	124	0.13%
KB7:	Jayne Hunt	0	8	0	0	0	0	0	0	8	0.01%
KB8:	Rick Richmond	1	0	0	0	4	0	1	0	6	0.01%
KB11:	Sally Palmer	27	23	0	10	200	6	6	206	478	0.50%
KB12:	Emmitt Kraft	0	1	0	1	0	0	0	0	2	0.00%
KB13:	AuxSvcs Orders	1	5	0	0	92	0	0	79	177	0.19%
KB16:	PIO #2	0	0	0	0	4	0	2	1	7	0.01%
KB18:	East Br check	0	193	1	0	11	0	0	11	216	0.23%
KB20:	Catalog I	0	0	1	0	1	0	0	0	2	0.00%
KB21:	East Br INFO	104	49	7	1	2086	0	297	778	3322	3.48%
KB23:	AuxSvcs Ibuild	1	14	0	0	7	0	2	8	32	0.03%
KB24:	Billing Divn	0	512	0	2	18	0	1	7	540	0.57%
KB25:	Core I	54	1	0	2	831	0	15	509	1412	1.48%
KB26:	Patron Regis	2	135	0	0	53	0	0	5	195	0.20%
KB27:	Book Return	1	15	0	0	36	0	0	2	54	0.06%
KB28:	Chargeout E	0	3	0	0	0	0	0	0	3	0.00%
KB29:	Chargeout W	3	0	0	0	7	0	4	13	27	0.03%
KB30:	300 baud dialup	51	4	8	56	556	2	60	32	769	0.81%
KB31:	300 baud dialup	33	1	2	16	382	0	45	58	537	0.56%
KB32:	300 baud dialup	16	1	0	17	153	0	24	9	220	0.23%
KB33:	300 baud dialup	0	0	0	1	0	0	5	0	6	0.01%
KB34:	300 baud dialup	1	0	0	0	3	0	8	3	15	0.02%
KB38:	INFO East	177	1	9	3	2402	1	148	699	3440	3.60%
KB39:	REFER South	49	2	8	11	1166	0	126	403	1765	1.85%
KB40:	N MOD office	2	0	0	1	191	0	11	480	685	0.72%
KB41:	INFO West	57	0	14	8	1335	0	168	649	2231	2.34%
KB43:	AuxSvcs Mod 1	0	0	1	0	71	0	0	6	78	0.08%
KB44:	Reserves	14	149	18	0	1128	0	1	328	1638	1.71%
KB45:	AuxSvcs Ibuild	1	0	2	0	22	0	0	4	29	0.03%
KB46:	Periodicals Off	2	1	0	0	49	0	0	56	108	0.11%
KB47:	Reference	56	3	13	8	1484	0	162	635	2361	2.47%
KB48:	Reserves	25	73	8	0	1418	0	0	434	1958	2.05%
KB49:	AuxSvcs Ibuild	0	14	0	0	2	0	0	2	18	0.02%
KB50:	Local History	11	0	0	0	69	0	12	25	117	0.12%
KB53:	Ute Pass Branch	8	1	1	0	95	0	2	39	146	0.15%
KB56:	Calhan Branch	1	24	0	1	60	0	2	35	123	0.13%
KB57:	Monument Branch	21	17	0	0	257	0	6	43	344	0.36%
KB58:	Fountain Branch	3	1	0	0	111	0	4	20	139	0.15%
KB59:	Old Colo City B	59	125	13	0	1371	0	32	264	1864	1.95%
KB60:	Broadmkt Branch	21	14	0	0	379	0	5	129	548	0.57%
KB61:	East Br CHARGE	2	38	0	0	27	0	0	3	70	0.07%
KB62:	Palmer Lk Branch	8	8	0	0	227	0	10	19	272	0.28%
KB63:	AuxSvcs Ibuild	4	3	0	0	24	0	0	7	38	0.04%
KB64:	Basement CheckIn	2	1	0	2	60	0	7	6	78	0.08%
KB66:	RideFinders	1	0	0	0	48	0	3	14	66	0.07%
KB68:	Mr. Dowlin	2	0	0	10	26	0	2	3	43	0.05%
KB69:	Gail Stowe	0	0	0	0	109	0	13	17	139	0.15%
KB72:	Interlib loan	5	5	1	3	24	0	7	7	52	0.05%
KB73:	Outreach	29	3	2	1	940	0	45	225	1245	1.30%
KB77:	Mrs. Sheff	9	9	3	8	612	0	11	343	995	1.04%

Fig. 11. Report of Online Catalog Use Statistics for the PPLD

Fig. 11—*Continued*

	1	2	3	4	5	6	7	8	9	10
KB78: Catalog II	8	5	1	0	72	0	0	34	120	0.13%
KB80: East Public 1	235	7	47	94	2738	10	948	638	4717	4.94%
KB81: East Public YA	231	13	35	79	2264	6	725	394	3747	3.92%
KB82: Public Children	202	14	39	110	2145	10	526	581	3627	3.80%
KB83: Sys Off spare	3	0	0	0	46	0	9	1	59	0.06%
KB85: Public S1	390	44	123	219	4748	24	1088	656	7292	7.63%
KB86: Public COCIS	18	4	6	12	506	1	140	67	754	0.79%
KB87: Public S3	404	21	150	141	3698	13	1049	565	6041	6.32%
KB89: Public N2	391	41	71	151	4982	19	1353	706	7719	8.08%
KB90: Public N3	293	27	61	108	3760	11	1078	478	5816	6.09%
KB91: Vivian Hurley	0	0	0	0	3	0	0	3	6	0.01%
KB92: Children's	16	3	0	2	714	0	10	175	920	0.96%
KB93: Bsmt Diablo	1	0	0	1	3	0	1	1	7	0.01%
KB94: YA Public 2	180	35	49	182	2579	24	709	454	4212	4.41%
KB96: YA Public 1	181	15	52	111	2096	14	726	384	3579	3.75%
KB97: West Public 1	226	23	77	161	2595	25	684	420	4211	4.41%
KB98: Public S2	410	26	133	139	3933	18	1146	655	6460	6.76%
KB99: Public N4	362	27	93	160	4032	15	1143	601	6433	6.73%
KB100: Core 11	1	1	0	0	231	0	0	102	335	0.35%
Totals	4540	1780	1064	1895	59581	217	12648	13799	95524	100.00%
Percentages	4.75%	1.86%	1.11%	1.98%	62.37%	0.23%	13.24%	14.45%	100.00%	100.00%

CODE

```
 1 = Author Search
 2 = Barcode Search
 3 = Dewey # Search
 4 = Expand Command
 5 = Fwd/Next Command
 6 = ICCN Search
 7 = Subject Search
 8 = Title Search
 9 - Total Commands
10 = Percent
```

Critical Incidents. These are reports on activities or incidents of the library employees that reflect favorably or unfavorably on the library. They are added to the employees file after the appropriate action is taken

Item Information. The online inventory provides information on each individual item in the computer. Figure 12 shows a search by subject, followed by a request for the full MARC record. Also shown is a search by title and author, moving forward in the file and requesting the next record.

Materials Encumbrances. The acquisition system generates a report once a month that lists all encumbrances from the materials budget. This report is broken down by type of item and department or division that placed the order. A report is shown in figure 13.

Information and Reference Detail Report. This is a report of the activities of the information services and reference division of public services. Figure 14 shows the report for March 1982.

```
PPL> S/FRONTIER AND PIONEER LIFE
Barcode:101160026      Patron:000000000        DueDate:None
                HUNTINGTON                     LastUse:21-Jan-82
917.98          ON THE EDGE OF NOWHERE
H9510           LCCN:66-026161                 InvDate:13-Dec-79
Monument Branch                                TotCirc:3
Subjects: Frontier and pioneer life - Alaska.
PPL> E/


010     66-026161
050   1 F909.H95
082     917.9803
099     917.98 H9510
100  10 Huntington, James, @d 1915 or 16-
245  10 On the edge of nowhere, @c by James Huntington, as told to Lawrence Elliott.
260   0 New York, @b Crown Publishers @c [1966]
300     vi, 183 p. @c 22 cm.
500     Autobiography.
650   0 Frontier and pioneer life @z  Alaska.
700  10 Elliott, Lawrence.
PPL> T/CUJO
Barcode:104185327      Patron:400145272        DueDate:20-Apr-82
N          KING,STEPH      Checked Out         LastUse:30-Mar-82
   .       CUJO
MCN        LCCN:81-050265                       InvDate:12-Sep-81
Penrose (Main)                                 TotCirc:10
PPL> A/BLUME,JUDY
Barcode:103537817      Patron:000000000        DueDate:None
YP         BLUME,JUDY                           LastUse:02-Apr-82
   .       FOREVER
           LCCN:74--22850                       InvDate:11-Jul-80
Old Colo City                                  TotCirc:7
PPL> F/
Barcode:101707404      Patron:400000006        DueDate:None
J          BLUME,JUDY                           LastUse:13-Dec-78
   .       DEENIE
B          LCCN:73-080197                       InvDate:30-Jan-79
Missing (PI81)                                 TotCirc:0
PPL> F/
Barcode:102434081      Patron:400992137        DueDate:28-Apr-82
J          BLUME,JUDY      Checked Out         LastUse:07-Apr-82
   .       DEENIE
B          LCCN:73-080197                       InvDate:29-May-79
Penrose (Main)                                 TotCirc:13
PPL> N/
Barcode:100781871      Patron:000000000        DueDate:None
           BLUMENAU,L                           LastUse:17-Feb-82
746.3      CREATIVE DESIGN IN WALL HANGINGS
B658C      LCCN:66-026169                       InvDate:12-Mar-79
Penrose (Main)                                 TotCirc:2
Subjects: Hand weaving.
          Wall hangings.
          Textile design.
PPL> X/
```

Fig. 12. Sample of the Item Information Report for the PPLD

Summary Report -- Line Items

Leased Books	:$ 7,546.25
Books	:$40,352.13
Microforms	:$ 39.00
Subscriptions	:$ 77.20
Standing Orders	:$ 3,609.57
Films & Filmstrips	:$ 444.23
Binding	:$ 0.00
Recordings	:$ 82.75
Framed Prints	:$ 0.00
Preview Materials	:$12,495.33
Unknown Lineitem	:$ 0.00

Summary Report -- File Totals

Total volumes in file	: 53,547
Encumbered volumes in file:	19,547
Unencumbered vol. in file	: 34,000
Total encumbered funds	:$64,646.46
Mean price per unenc. vol.:	$ 3.30

Fig. 13. Materials Budget Encumbrances Report for the PPLD

Figure 13—*Continued*

Summary Report -- Department & Division

RE / AD	$20,565.20
EX / EA	$ 5,110.44
FL / MU	$ 2,428.17
CH / AD	$10,051.34
LO / AD	$ 3,593.48
FL / GI	$ 1,371.33
OU / BO	$ 514.85
EX / BR	$ 1,186.15
EX / UT	$ 821.48
EX / MO	$ 571.54
EX / JA	$ 813.80
AD / CO	$ 9,401.07
EX / OL	$ 1,833.30
IN / AD	$ 122.30
EX / FO	$ 330.40
EX / PA	$ 600.89
FL / CL	$ 2,058.12
EX / CA	$ 760.11
OU / AD	$ 968.28
FL / TR	$ 100.00
FL / HU	$ 430.20
FL / OT	$ 525.00
EX / AD	$ 35.45
AU / CA	$ 355.00
FL / PL	$ 83.00
FL / CO	$ 15.50

```
 1.  Questions Answered-Directional                                    356
 2.  Questions Answered-Search-Phone                                 2,305
 3.  Questions answered-Search-Walk-in                               2,428
       TOTAL number of search questions                             4,733

 4.  Number of tours
 5.  People at tours
 6.  Programs
 7.  People at programs
 8.  Outside contacts
 9.  People contacted outside
10.  Local data base accesses                                       1,771

10A. Non-local data base accesses

11.  Courses-Number of items added                                  1,450
12.  Courses-Number of items modified                                  15
13.  Courses-Number of items deleted                                1,340
13A. Courses-Corrections made                                           7
14.  Courses-Keywords accessed                                        139
15.  Courses-Agencies' input hours                                      0
16.  Courses-Total number of courses at the end of each month       3,059

17.  Clubs-Number of Clubs added                                        5
18.  Clubs-Number of Clubs modified                                    33
19.  Clubs-Number of Clubs deleted                                      1
19A. Clubs-Number of corrections made                                   0
20.  Clubs-Names accessed                                             562
21.  Clubs-Keywords accessed                                          254
22.  Clubs-Total number of clubs at the end of each month             581
22A. Clubs-Printouts sold                                               4

23.  Call-Number of agencies added                                      7
24.  Call-Number of agencies modified                                  45
25.  Call-Number of agencies deleted                                    6
25A. Call-Number of corrections made                                    0
26.  Call-Agencies accessed                                           562
27.  Call-Keywords accessed                                           254
28.  Call-Total number of agencies at the end of each month           684
28A. Call-Printouts sold                                                2

29.  COCIS and GIS printouts                                            8
29A. Partial Call and Calendar printouts                               70

30.  Community Events Calendars mailed                                240
31.  Calendar items added                                             139
32.  Calendar items modified                                            9
32A. Calendar items corrected                                           7
33.  Calendar items deleted                                           208
33A. Calendar-Keywords accessed                                        --
33B. Calendar-Total number of events at the end of each month         190
33C. Calendar-Total number of current subscribers                      68
```

Fig. 14. Report Generated for Statistics for Information Services
and Reference for the PPLD

Fig. 14—*Continued*

44. Business Info added

52. Day Care-Agencies added
53. Day Care-Agencies deleted
54. Day Care-Agencies modified
54A. Day Care-Corrections made
55. Day Care-Total number of Agencies (Homes) at the end of each month
55A. Day Care-Keywords accessed

Total volunteer hours--report

Periodicals Use Study. This report is a study of the use of current subscriptions, and is made three times a year for a two week period to provide data for subscription renewal. A partial display of this study is shown in figure 15.

Challenged Material. Complaints from the public on the appropriateness of library material are received on the form provided. Receipt of this form initiates the procedure for reevaluation of material.

Interlibrary Loan Report. This report is not automated at this time, but will be in the near future.

Patron Information. The circulation system stores information about the persons who register. A sample of this program is shown in figure 16.

Project Status Reports. These reports are usually required by external agencies. Examples are the quarterly reports required by the National Endowment for the Humanities, the state library, etc.

The DSS includes utility programs to provide several types of statistical analysis including means, standard deviations and Pearson r (the Pearson product-moment correlation coefficient r test). In addition, the library has used the Statistical Package for the Social Sciences (SPSS) on the University of Colorado's computer in Boulder. This program can be accessed directly from one of our library terminals. A vendor-supplied program for financial modeling was tried; and it was found that it was too specific for our purposes and would not adapt easily to the type of statistics collected and analyzed by the library. Another vendor-supplied program, which calculates Beysian formulas and probability, has been received; but the library has been unable to load the program into its Radio Shack Model II computer. Investigation will continue for a program that will translate the data or collections of data contained in the DSS automatically into charts and/or graphs. One program was located that appears to do this, but the license cost is $60,000. Since we believe that the cost of a program

TITLE	COST	USE	INDEX	OTHER SUBSCRIBERS
Administrative Management	16	1	BPI	AFA
Aging	9.25	1	RG	-
Alaska	18	3	Access	-
Alternative Sources of Energy	20	1	-	CC
American Artist	17	2	RG,PAIS	UCCS
American city and County	30	1	RG	CC,AFA
American Education	12	1	RG	CC,AFA,UCCS
American History Illus.	15	2	RG	AFA
Americana	11.90	1	RG	AFA
Americas	12	1	RG	CC,UCCS,AFA
Antiques	33	2	RG	-
Antiques Journal	11	1	RG	-
Architectural Digest	36	3	Access	-
Arizona Highways	12	1	Access	CC,AFA
Art News	20	4	RG	CC,AFA,UCCS
Astronautics and Aeronautics	42	1	ASTI	AFA
Astronomy	16	4	RG	CC,AFA,UCCS
Atlantic Monthly	18	1	RG	CC,UCCS,AFA
Audio	11.94	5	ASTI	AFA
Audubon Magazine	13	2	RG	CC,AFA
Aviation week and Space Tech	45	9	RG,MI,BPI	AFA,UCCS
Backpacker	15	6	Access	CC,AFA,UCCS
Better Homes and Gardens	10	2	RG	-
Bicycling	11.80	3	Access	CC
Billboard	110	3	-	AFA
Black Enterprise	10	2	RG	-
Black Stars	10	3	-	-

Fig. 15. Periodicals Use Study for the PPLD

DOE, JOHN G

400993887 DOE, JOHN G
4741 E KIOWA
Phone: 474-2255   Zip: 80909
Out: 000   Ovr: 000   Fines: 001.10
New: 08-Dec-79   Last: 06-Nov-81
          Flags (DSCLZX): <P4   M>
Note: 100.01.23.2R

Function (A,D,F,M,N,S,X):

401414933 DOE, JOHN G
1222 N KIOWA AV
Phone: 473-2222   Zip: 80909
Out: 000   Ovr: 000   Fines: .
New: 19-Oct-81   Last: 19-Oct-81
          Flags (DSCLZX): <P   M>
Note:

Function (A,D,F,M,N,S,X):

401414917 DOE, JOHN G
4420 E ASPEN DR
Phone: 444-2263   Zip: 80901
Out: 000   Ovr: 000   Fines: .
New: 19-Oct-81   Last: 19-Oct-81
          Flags (DSCLZX): <P3 L M>
Note: RL 10.01.81

Function (A,D,F,M,N,S,X):

401414891 DOE, JOHN G
2230 E KIOWA
Phone: 473-2241   Zip: 80909
Out: 000   Ovr: 000   Fines: .
New: 19-Oct-81   Last: 19-Oct-81
          Flags (DSCLZX): <P3 L M>
Note: BILL

Function (A,D,F,M,N,S,X):

401414925 DOE, JOHN G
4420 E KIOWA AV
Phone: 473-2266   Zip: 80212
Out: 000   Ovr: 000   Fines: .
New: 19-Oct-81   Last: 19-Oct-81
          Flags (DSCLZX): <P1F M>
Note: INDEBTEDNESS

Function (A,D,F,M,N,S,X): X

                    Circulation Department
                         > Menu <
                  For HELP enter "?selection"

        EXIT   CHECK   GOODBYE   BKSOUT

Fig. 16. Patron Information Report for the PPLD

should not exceed its value to the library, we declined to purchase this program.

The goal for the DSS is for the library director or the manager to use a terminal to ask the DSS: How is the library today? The system would respond with such comments as: "terrible," "lousy," "fair," "good," "not bad," or "great." The questioner could then ask why. The system would respond with a summary report of all of the indicators using predefined criteria that would indicate exceptions. I believe that this is possible to do for the system. The major tasks are to define the relevance of the indicators and the criteria used to isolate exceptions to the norm. The Pikes Peak Library District will continue to use the DSS as a management tool. It has progressed far beyond the stage of just collecting numbers.

REFERENCES

1. Taggart, Marvin M., Jr., and Tharp, Marvin O. "Dimensions of Information Requirements Analysis." *Data Base* 7(Summer 1975):8.

2. Schoderbek, Peter P., et al. *Management Systems: Conceptual Considerations*, rev. ed. Dallas, Tex.: Business Publications, 1980, p. 8.

3. Cheney, Paul H., and Dickson, Gary W. "Organizational Characteristics and Information Systems: An Exploratory Investigation." *Academy of Management Journal* 25(March 1982):181-82.

4. Anthony, Robert N. *Planning and Control Systems: A Framework for Analysis.* Boston: Harvard University, 1965, p. 14.

5. Wagner, Gerald R. "Decision Support in the Office of the Future." *Managerial Planning* 28(May/June 1980):3-5.

6. Seaman, John. "Coping with the Coming Big Changes—Part I." *Computer Decisions* 12(Sept. 1980):76.

7. Keen, Peter, and Morton, Michael S. *Decision Support Systems: An Organizational Perspective.* Reading, Mass.: Addison-Wesley Publishing Co., 1978, p. 1.

8. Zani, William M. "Blueprint for MIS." *Harvard Business Review* 48(Nov./Dec 1970):100.

9. Dowlin, Kenneth E. *The Promise of the Electronic Library.* New York: Neil Schuman Press, 1982.

10. Brown, Maryann K. "Library Data, Statistics, and Information: Progress Toward Comparability." *Special Libraries* 71(Nov. 1980):475-84.

11. Library Administration and Management Association. *Library Effectiveness: A State of the Art.* New York: LAMA, ALA, 1980.

12. Community Planning and Research Council. *The Pikes Peak Library in the 1980's: A Plan for Development.* Colorado Springs, Colo.: CPRC, 1979.

KATHLEEN M. HEIM
Assistant Professor
Graduate School of Library and Information Science
University of Illinois at Urbana-Champaign

Organizational Considerations Relating to the Implementation and Use of Management Information Systems

A management information system (MIS) is the process and structure used by an organization to identify, collect, evaluate, transfer, and utilize information in order to fulfill its objectives. It is a system that provides management with information to make decisions, evaluate alternatives, measure performance, and detect situations requiring corrective action.[1]

For library managers to utilize an MIS in their operations, precise and well-defined data categories are required as Runyon points out in his discussion of the need for systems to assemble elusive and fugitive library statistical measures.[2] Bommer and Chorba (1982) have described the use of MIS for academic and special libraries in a more highly evolved mode— that of a decision support system—with detailed consideration of management reporting as a means of better identification of the activities, problems and needs of users.[3] Dowlin (1980 and in these proceedings) has consistently presented examples of evermore refined "up-and-running" MIS in library settings with an emphasis on system components and decision-making.[4]

Most of the discussions addressing the use of MIS in libraries have, by necessity, focused on functional areas or subsystems which affect the dynamics of information and new knowledge in the following ways:

> (a) stored data relations, (b) system known logical relations, (c) program defined logical relations, (d) algorithm defined logical relations, and (e) end-user perceived logical relations. The intent of an MIS is to provide the knowledge (the correct knowledge) with which to efficiently/ effectively operate a system. A system can be defined as a library, a private corporation, a local government, etc.[5]

This requisite focus on the integration of functional areas within a large system in the early stages of MIS implementation fails, somewhat, to consider impacts of an MIS on the organization *qua* organization and on those who work in it.

This discussion will focus on organizational aspects of MIS implementation and use rather than on technical or functional issues. Because few library examples of fully developed MIS exist we must turn to state-of-the-art analyses of these systems' impact on organizational structure and process which are lodged mainly in corporate or industrial discussions. However, just as many of the principles of administrative theory formulated for business enterprises are translatable, with modification, to the nonprofit sector, so much of what is known about MIS deployment can be similarly extrapolated for library considerations. In this respect we are fortunate perhaps in that the slowness of libraries to recognize the managerial implications of information generated by electronic data processing systems has meant that we should be able to anticipate the problems which will arise and work to circumvent them before library MIS systems are more fully developed.

Organization Variables Affecting MIS Acceptance

Before we examine the effect of MIS on organizations once they are in place, it is important to understand the organizational variables which may affect the initial acceptance of these systems. Ein-dor and Segev (1978) have characterized these variables as uncontrollable, partially controllable and controlled.[6]

Uncontrollable variables include organizational size, structure at the time of implementation, time frame, and the extraorganizational situation. Larger organizations have found greater success with MIS use than smaller ones. Libraries, even the largest, are relatively small organizations and much planning is required to initiate and gain acceptance of MIS. There will be more resistance in small organizations than in very large ones since the likelihood of a lesser degree of bureaucratization and traditional line and staff authority divisions are in place in such operations. The perception of the MIS as crystallizing these divisions may offset their initial acceptance.

The more decentralized the organization at the time of MIS initiation or consolidation of various components into a single system, the less likely there will be a warm reception to their consolidation. This situation is an important one for library planners. Independent systems for various functions are not easy to combine, and since each is accompanied in its own context by its own analysts, programmers and goals, the organization may face difficulty at the time the decision to merge the systems is made. That is, separate acquisition, bibliographic control and circulation systems will not merge easily if they are already independent entities and may compete for funds. Incongruity between MIS and organizational time frames also militates against acceptance of the MIS. This is a problem for production-oriented organizations but may also be seen to occur in some library situations as well. Generally the more relaxed the organization in terms of time constraints, the easier MIS implementation will be. For example, the dreaded "closing of the catalog" proclamations made throughout the nation filled users and librarians with foreboding and doom. Such time-frame constraints create more dissension than a more relaxed initiation of systems that are more easily integrated at the organization's natural pace.

External factors such as the availability of resources for MIS implementation are also important. The organization with adequate data processing personnel or ease of access to these people will experience greater success than the organization that finds these resources difficult to marshall. The library that must hire programmers and data entry personnel from outside its own ranks will not only find difficulty in conveying its needs to these "outsiders" but may not be able to sustain upgrading and system maintenance. For those institutions outside of metropolitan areas it will most likely be necessary to shift some personnel to permanent posts in system maintenance—a reallocation of resources with possible negative personnel impact if done without adequate planning or anticipation.

Partially controllable variables include budgeting of organizational resources, organizational maturity and the psychological climate of the organization. Prior to implementation it is difficult for MIS to assume imaginable cost/benefit analysis. Since they may not clearly "cost out," they can only be initiated by managers with a great deal of insight. Rather than mount an entire system it has been easier, especially in libraries, to implement subsystems with the concomitant difficulties of consolidation at the time that the full-blown MIS is desired.

Maturity of an organization is usually defined as the degree to which systems are formalized, quantified and producing data appropriate to decision and control. They are rational and formal. The more mature an organization the more likely the MIS will be accepted since it will continue the generation of these data.

The psychological climate of an organization vis-à-vis MIS is the amount of expectation for the system. Most expect too much from such systems at the outset, and when magical formulas for decision-making do not spew forth, retreat from the system on the supposition that it has been oversold. Others have heard terrible stories about MIS and bring negative feelings to their implementation. The best environment for effective organizational success with an MIS is one in which preconceptions are weak and realistic expectations can be developed.

Fully controllable variables include rank and location of the executive and advisory committees responsible for the MIS. The more highly placed the individual or committee to whom the MIS developers report, the greater the likelihood of organizational acceptance. It has been found that if this is more than two levels below the top of the organizational hierarchy the likelihood of success is reduced. A high level steering committee to guide MIS efforts, establish policy, identify potentially valuable projects, and recommend resource allocations has been viewed as fundamental to its acceptance.

The nature of library implementation of subsystem MIS, rather than overall systems developed for general decision-making, render it difficult to require that planners step back and examine the likelihood of success insofar as the above factors are concerned. Given the organizational variables which accommodate or impede MIS acceptance and success, it seems that libraries and systems with the following characteristics will find MIS most compatible: those which are large; centralized; have no tight time frames for the accomplishment of goals; can employ an adequate supply of system personnel; have few budget problems; are already formed and geared to statistics gathering and have no strong preconceptions of how an MIS should be. The top executive will be fully committed to the system which was planned by a steering committee and is monitored by and responsible to a highly placed individual within the organization. Although few libraries will fit this profile, recognition of these variables may increase the capacity of system planners to understand partial failures or resistance to acceptance of MIS.

MIS and Organizational Effect

The general literature of MIS and organizational effect takes two main viewpoints: (1) implications for organizational structure and processes; and (2) implications for managerial performance at various levels of administration. For each of these we will identify aspects of special pertinence to the library and information center context.

Implications for Organizational Structure and Processes

Change in the Shape of Organizations

Although there are many ways to describe organizational structure and many variants on the generally accepted pyramidal model, it is helpful to imagine such a model in order to discuss current thinking on the effect of MIS on traditional organizations. In such a model there are three basic managerial levels: *top management,* whose tasks are development of the organization's domain, management of the interface with external environments, and establishment of the organization's administrative climate; *middle management,* which develops rules, procedures and policies in order to interpret them to fit day-to-day operations; and *technical management,* which sees that services are rendered and policies carried out. In addition to this vertical model, horizontal differential may also take place in varying degrees.

In libraries, horizontal specialization is nearly always functional since this provides for clear task assignments and the exercise of expert technical skills. A problem with this sort of horizontal development is the tendency of individual units to develop their own complex communication channels with no gangplank mechanisms among units. This usually forces coordination to the top of the organization where functional concerns merge. Given this tendency, there is a natural assumption that the implementation of an MIS system would concentrate greater power at the organization's upper strata and isolate individual units.

It is not a consideration here whether or not the way libraries are organized is efficient or effective. The main question is whether or not the implementation of an MIS will fundamentally alter whatever organizational model is in place at the time of implementation. As yet no clear consensus has emerged about the impact of MIS on organizational structure. In their review of the literature on organizational structure and MIS, Ignizio and Shannon (1971) identified two main camps: those who felt that MIS would cause development of an hourglass organization with more top managers, fewer middle managers and a greater ratio of skilled to unskilled workers; and those who felt that the pyramid structure would bulge with more management levels.[7] Not unexpectedly, more recent observers anticipate that the MIS will become the binding force in organizations as its use demonstrates the weaknesses of older structured forms and becomes the model for new organizational design.*

Centralization v. Decentralization

The most hotly debated question concerning the impact of MIS on organizational structure has been whether they will lead to more or less centralization. Since World War II, organizations have grown more complex and this, coupled with a human resources orientation on the part of management, has meant a tendency to decentralize. However, since MIS

---

*As one interested in the professionalization process it gave me some cheer to see the MIS people struggling with the problems of more mature professions vis-à-vis their own status and prestige. The exhortations of management writers that MIS technologists become integrated into their organizations seems to be one these technicians are resisting—after all, once one has received holy orders is it ever possible to become one of the congregation?

provide the complicated organizational communication systems required to maintain control, and lessen the need to delegate authority through reduction of time needed to assimilate feedback information, it is likely that recentralization may occur. The reduction and regrouping of middle levels of management, usually accompanying MIS implementation, also contributes to recentralization.

Situational factors may be the critical component in this issue. While economy of operation may be gained through concentration of information at the top levels of the organization, resistance on the part of an educated work force for whom creativity may be a greater satisfaction than other motivational considerations, can slow this process. The initial desirability of concentrating information at the top of an organization may thus be outweighed by the need to develop a corps of managers-in-training who have had decision-making experience as well as by recognition of the demoralizing effects of inhibiting those at lower managerial levels from exercising discretion and judgment. In an organization of professionals such as a library, it is dangerous to hoard control over management information. The MIS is a tool which can be used as easily for centralization as for decentralization depending upon which direction the initiators of the system wish the organization to move. Given the strong indications of behavioral research that attest to the needs of professionals to maintain autonomy and decision-making capability in order to derive satisfaction from their work, it would seem unwise for any MIS system which totally circumvents those whose technical expertise is needed by the organization to be installed unless these individuals are seen as replaceable. It is not the MIS which creates consolidation of power but those in charge of developing the system's use patterns. Federico (1980) has pointed out, in his analysis of this issue, that the motivation and performance of middle managers can suffer if the shift in control toward the top is perceived as threatening the accountability and authority of middle managers.[8]

Change in Control

For those top managers with an inclination to share power and control of decisions, the MIS may actually make this process more palatable. Since an MIS allows monitoring of decisions, a manager inclined to share power may do so and continue to monitor the outcome with a capacity to determine if a subordinate has acted in an acceptable manner. Those reluctant to release authority could be apprised of the context in which decisions are made at lower levels and be reassured as to their appropriateness. Traditional organizational dependence on coercive power can be lessened with the implementation of an MIS since, theoretically, information could be shared by those in the best position to use it. Argyris (1982) has hypothesized the development of a project team or matrix form of organization designed around relevant information rather than formal power.[9] Peer relationship might be emphasized and members of matrix groups assigned equal power to make decisions with the ultimate result a lessening of superior/subordinate identification. The potential for participatory management and maturity of the individuals in an organization could then be enhanced.

Such a development, however, will call for a new breed of executive officer at the top of an organization. If competence and technical knowledge replace formal authority, those top managers who maintain control by withholding information will find themselves less powerful and less essential. The MIS, if used openly, could cause a major organizational restructuring from arbitrariness to explicitness.

The three impacts of MIS on organizational structure so far discussed: (1) change in shape of the organization, (2) centralization *v.* decentralization, and (3) change in the control and authority structure of the organization do not happen in isolation. As we have already pointed out the attitude of top management toward the use of MIS may alter the direction taken vis-à-vis these three impacts.

Alteration of Organizational Processes

MIS alter organizational processes as well as organizational structure. The large general literature on "change" and change agents is helpful in understanding means to mitigate the effects of MIS installation. Foresight into potential organizational transformation is difficult, but Federico discusses axioms of alteration such as those developed by Benne and Birnbaum to mitigate the negative affects of MIS implementation. These include:

1. changing of all relevant aspects of the system (not just obvious ones);
2. *complementary* and *reinforcing* changes on all levels;
3. introduction of change at stress points since these are the areas most amenable to modification;
4. consideration of informal as well as formal organizations; and
5. inclusion of those affected in the planning of the change.[10]

Organizational acumen is a key factor in MIS implementation. Anticipation of the variety of organizational impacts and action to develop balances in the new system are crucial.

Change in organizational processes introduced may be examined at both the individual and general personnel levels. At the individual level, Coleman and Riley (1972) have noted that change caused by MIS creates conflict and stress which generates resistance arising from inaccurate perceptions of the effect of the MIS on the organization—fear of the unknown; anxiety arising from enlarged responsibility; threat to position and stature; and disruption of personal relations.[11] Petroff (1973) has added the fear of more precise personnel evaluation.[12]

The literature concerning the effects of MIS on general personnel issues includes discussion of changes in job content, task requirements and retraining. While upper management may experience broadening and increased responsibility, jobs lower in the organization may become more routine and reduced in content. In fact, those higher in the organization have indicated more satisfaction with MIS than those lower.[13] At clerical and supervisory levels, interpersonal relation skills become less important while at the higher levels more openness is required. These effects may find the organization with a highly efficient MIS to have two different administrative philosophies in operation: a near return to Taylorism at the lower levels and an extreme case of human resources orientation at the higher levels. Since these styles tend to be antithetical, very real personnel problems may develop. A number of MIS analysts agree that personnel problems associated with MIS implementation cause more disappointments and failures than technical problems. In an organization composed of a great many professionals, the need for creativity and individuality are high. Insofar as an MIS may concentrate these job requirements at a few levels, important motivators may be removed from the workplace.

The threat of depersonalization and personnel perceptions that their positions have been reduced to MIS—created niches reflecting only the needs of the system rather than the employee, rank high in the list of problems which face the organization attempting to implement an MIS. Libraries are particularly susceptible to this problem since low salaries mandate that those employed derive greater nonhygienic benefits in order to sustain motivation. Removal of motivational factors, most libraries' only means of providing job satisfaction, may undermine the rationale for staying on the job. Finally, one rather short-term effect of the MIS on organizational processes must be noted. In the introductory stages an MIS will cause lags in the organization's progress. Routines that were relatively efficient, or seemed to be so, will be disrupted as new ones are introduced.[14] While this effect should be overcome as the system becomes familiar to employees, short-term major disruptions will generate ill will toward the new system unless they have been well prepared for.

The three main impacts of MIS on organizational processes are: (1) radical change, (2) individual and general personnel dissatisfaction as job content is revised and new task clusters evolve, and (3) disruption of routine. If anticipated and planned for, these can be minimized, but if MIS are introduced without adequate attention to these factors the system may have difficulty due to personnel resistance.

Implications of MIS for Management

The most salient question regarding MIS and its effect on management is whether an MIS will fundamentally alter managerial functions as they are practiced. If an erosion of traditional management responsibilities occurs with MIS implementation, the general conception of what comprises management skills may well change. Most researchers agree that the effects of MIS will be very different on different levels of management. At the highest levels, managers with the support of an MIS should be able to focus more intensely on innovation and change, develop alternative simulations for problems to be solved, investigate up-to-date research findings, avoid routine decision-making, and shunt organizational loyalty considerations in favor of more rational concerns with difficult problems.[15] Middle managers, on the other hand, could find their work more highly structured and reduced in status. The truncation of the middle manager role would require more specialization and less scope of action. We have already seen in our discussion of the effects of the MIS on the structure of the organization that the role of the middle manager could go either way.

This potential change in the practice of management is ironic in the face of recent investigations of the styles of administration in Japanese firms with their focus on maximization of human resources. Since a central factor in the success of these firms is in their commitment to the consultative style of decision-making, structured to involve the whole group rather than a few individuals, the implementation of MIS in terms of organizational behavior and shifts in managerial style may move us farther from the successful modes of management and back into an earlier more centralized phase.

Elsewhere in these proceedings, Olsgaard addresses factors involved in top management's use or nonuse of information so we will comment here primarily on effects of an MIS at lower levels in the organizational hierarchy.

The horizontal effects of MIS implementation are of special importance when trying to assess the role of the MIS at lower levels of management. The MIS as an integrated computer-based system for providing information to support operations and decision-making tends to be quite useful at middle-management levels if in fact a more flexible view of an MIS is understood in its operational mode.

The more information available to a manager, the more involved she/he will be in her/his commitment to the organization's goals. The traditional functional division of library operations without solid interdepartmental communication gangplanks can cause isolation and power hoarding in individual units. Since an integrated MIS could conceivably open a system and enable qualified users to peruse various aspects of the operation tangential to the designated area of concern, the context of individual decisions might be made with a better understanding of where the organization is at any given point. An MIS will facilitate horizontal communication since it will force consistent definitions and formats. Interdependence of units should increase.

In a library setting all this is speculation since, in a service organization with rather pure missions and goals, considerations of unit power and control should be moot. Ideally there would be no need to wrest power or importance for a particular unit since goals should be kept in mind more consistently through such devices as the planning process for public libraries or frequent analyses of objectives via MRAP (Management Review and Analysis Program)[16] in academic settings.

However, the rise of MIS has seen a shift, perhaps a short-term one, but nevertheless a shift, in perceptions of unit power in larger libraries. Prestige and status accrue to those who work in departments with greater MIS capabilities. The old technical/public services dichotomy, with the implicit emphasis on public service, has blurred and the action, the excitement, the pioneering edge of librarianship seems now to be the realm of technical services. The increase of public service literature focusing on online searching or computer-assisted instruction (CAI) underscores this observation. The cachet which comes with synergistic innovation with a CRT seems to add prestige to those who work plugged into an electric keyboard. For the time being the technical services' development of MIS, both locally and through networking, is far ahead of those in the public services. These events may create a short term imbalance of departmental power and tempt units into competition—a dysfunctional situation for the organization's mission.

Saunders's examination of MIS and departmental power has some applicability to libraries. She defines power as the capability of a subunit through formal position or actual or perceived participation in organizational activities to exert influence on another subunit to act in a prescribed manner.[17] If subunits vie for scarce organizational resources, especially personnel, there must be mutual assessment of power bases. The ability of one department to exert influence on another is determined to the extent to which it participates in organizational decision-making on key organizational issues. These may change over time or be different for any given institution. An ARL library with its concentration on collection development and maintenance may find that the bibliographic units are more important than the public service units, especially if the administration is more committed to number of volumes and depth of collection than service. A library serving a research and development function, on the other hand, may be so committed to the support of research that the public service function takes precedence.

The use of an MIS may affect the power of units in three ways: (1) increased access to information may allow subunits greater influence in organizational decision-making on key issues; (2) the capacity to cope with uncertainty may also grant greater power within the organization to the degree to which the unpredictability ensuing from lack of information about future events may be reduced; and (3) the nonsubstitutability or difficulty with which the activities of a unit may be performed by an alternate department. These affect pervasiveness and number of linkages with other units.

Task criticalness and the degree to which the activities of a unit affect the achievement of the main goals of the organization is a mediating variable.[18] Depending upon the library's long term goals, task criticalness may shift and create deceptive short-term power imbalances within units. A good example is closure of the catalog. While one of the ultimate goals is provision of multiple access points, achievement of that goal has involved a series of changing power bases within the library. Hardware developers, software programmers, catalogers, and ultimately public service librarians have all participated in effective use of this tool. As tasks critical to the goal's success have changed, so has the relative power of units associated with each step. While this shift has short-term disruptive effects, the long-term goal will be met and, insofar as units subscribe to the organization's mission, competition avoided. Those responsible middle managers who experience shifts in power as various subunits rise and fall in their power base, must be ready to accept the changing perceived measure of status.

Since MIS can enhance the power of organizational units, another administration consideration must be how important power may be to managers. Job satisfaction studies which have demonstrated a positive correlation between employer performance and perceived status of the manager and the power of the unit should be considered in terms of changing unit dynamics due to the better availability of information. An MIS capacity to generate too much information, alluded to in the keynote speech, is also a determinant of employee satisfaction. O'Reilly (1980) has shown that perceptions of over- or underload correlate with satisfaction depending upon the manager's style.[19]

For the middle manager attuned to organizational goals, the effect of MIS can be quite positive. New communication patterns can be established, better decisions can be made, and more shared knowledge can be available. These factors could prove disruptive to the empire builder, however, since, in the long range, MIS should function to streamline the overall organization to the detriment of unit power, although short-term and somewhat misleading expansion of unit power may take place. From the larger organizational perspective, this evolutionary and dynamic nature of MIS's effect on middle management should be anticipated and planned for.

Conclusion

The potential of MIS for better organizational decision-making and better deployment of organizational resources is great. However, in libraries this capacity has generally been discussed without adequate attention to the complex factors of organizational structure and processes or the resultant effects on individuals; restructuring of institutional personnel policies; resultant shifts on the demands of top and middle management; or changes in unit to unit communication, power and satisfaction.

The voluminous literature on these aspects of MIS implementation in the general management literature are inconclusive and confusing. On either side of any issue a number of studies support the direction in which each of these organizational factors might move. However, as with any new innovation, the addition of MIS capacities to organizational life requires careful consideration of the human element in individual and group interaction. The lure of precision through information, economy through better understanding of quantifiable variables and efficiency through clearer analysis of service and production may so alter the organization that those in charge of the organization's direction may find its workers (both professional and support staff) confused, less satisfied and alienated.

Sterling (1980) has observed that MIS systems and their concentration of feasibility, workability and minimization of costs have failed to focus management concern on the antihuman aspects of such efforts.[20] Since automation of any management system codifies the rigidity of practice and expands it to ever larger circles, the prerogative to formulate questions important to the human element of the organization is diminished. In conclusion, I would like to caution that the glamour of MIS and their capacity for variant simulations of organizational outcomes be considered carefully in light of the human factors in an organization. The paucity of service organization studies makes their advancement into MIS implementation even more uncertain than in those that are profit based. We simply do not know what will happen but we must recognize that the human factor has played a role of great importance in libraries to date and not forego our investment in the development of a highly skilled and technically competent corps of professionals in favor of efficiency and streamlining of operations.

At this critical stage of MIS innovation, with seemingly unlimited technological opportunities, it is more important than ever before that the organizational and individual consequences be attended to, analyzed, and considered as major managerial adjustments involving MIS are undertaken.

REFERENCES

1. Morss, Elliott R., and Rich, Robert F. *Government Information Management: A Counter-Report of Commission of Federal Paperwork.* Boulder, Colo.: Westview Press, 1980, p. 137.

2. Robey, Daniel. "User Attitudes and Management Information System Use." *Academy of Management Journal* 22(Sept. 1979):527-38; and Runyon, Robert S. "Towards the Development of a Library Management Information System." *College & Research Libraries* 42(Nov. 1981):539-48.

3. Bommer, Michael R.W., and Chorba, Ronald W. *Decision Making for Library Management.* White Plains, N.Y.: Knowledge Industry Publications, 1982; and Bommer, Michael R.W., et al. "Performance Assessment Model for Academic Libraries." *Journal of the ASIS* 30(March 1979):93-99.

4. Dowlin, Kenneth E. "A Public Library Management System." In *Library Effectiveness: A State of the Art*, pp. 85-110. Chicago: ALA, 1980.

5. Mendiville to Heim, personal communication, 5 April 1982.

6. Ein-dor, Phillip, and Segev, Eli. "Organizational Context and the Success of Management Information Systems." *Management Science* 24(June 1978):1064-77.

7. Ignizio, J.P., and Shannon, R.E. "Organization Structures in the 1980's." *Industrial Engineering* 3(Sept. 1971):46-50.

8. Federico, Pat-Anthony, et al. *Management Information Systems and Organizational Behavior.* New York: Praeger, 1980.

9. Argyris, Chris. "Organizational Learning and Management Information Systems." *Data Base* 13(Winter/Spring 1982):3-11.

10. Federico, et al., *Management Information Systems,* p. 104.

11. Coleman, R.J., and Riley, M.J. "The Organizational Impact of MIS." *Journal of Systems Management* 23(March 1972):13-19.

12. Petroff, J.N. "Why are DP Managers So Unpopular?" *Datamation* 19(Feb. 1973):77-79.

13. Federico, et al. *Management Information Systems,* pp. 110-18.

14. Ibid., p. 160.

15. Ibid., p. 38.

16. For a review of MRAP see: Johnson, Edward R., and Mann, Stuart H. *Organization Development for Academic Libraries: An Evaluation of the Management Review and Analysis Program.* Westport, Conn.: Greenwood Press, 1980.

17. Saunders, Carol S. "Management Information Systems, Communications, and Departmental Power: An Integrative Model." *Academy of Management Review* 6(July 1981):433.

18. Ibid., p. 437.

19. O'Reilly, Charles A., III. "Individuals and Information Overload in Organizations: Is More Necessarily Better?" *Academy of Management Journal* 23(Dec. 1980):684-96.

20. Sterling, Theodore D. "Humanizing Computerized Information Systems." In *Management System in the Human Services*, edited by Murray L. Gruber, pp. 287-99. Philadelphia, Pa.: Temple University Press.

WAYNE MULLIN
Head Loan Librarian
University of Arizona Library

Geac as a Source of Management Information

When Professor Lancaster called to ask if I would be willing to give a paper on management aspects of the Geac Online Circulation System,* I was both elated and apprehensive because the University of Arizona was in the unique position of just having gone from a nonstandard version of Geac software to the standard 4.0 turnkey version. At the time I accepted the invitation, no one at the University of Arizona knew much about what management data Geac could provide. I am obliged to tell you straightaway that there is still much that we at Arizona do not know about the management data Geac can provide. But in the almost two years we have been on Geac, we have learned a thing or two—some of which relates to the topic of this Clinic.

Among the more interesting things learned was that Geac came in several "flavors," at least from June 1980 through June 1981. At installation and through the first year, ours was not "vanilla"—a pure turnkey system—but rather what came to be dubbed by us as "marble fudge." We think that we are the only marble fudge system in existence, but Geac would be a better source of this information than I. What I am saying is that our Geac 8000 looked, from the outside, like a turnkey Geac; performed somewhat like a turnkey Geac; but, oh boy, it sure didn't work and look like a turnkey Geac when one got inside the guts of the thing. The upshot of being marble fudge was that we did not have many reports until installation of the version 4.0 thirteen months after coming live.

---

*This paper describes the Geac Online Circulation System as it existed in March 1982. Readers should be aware that there have been numerous changes and improvements during the past year.

To fully appreciate—or at least to appreciate to some degree—what I will say this afternoon is to have some understanding of my background and the environment at the University of Arizona Library. First, I am a librarian. One of those people who got turned on to libraries from having worked in one as a support staff and I know well that some of you can talk circles around me when it comes to understanding how computers really work, or sometimes do not work at all. What I will cover then first is a librarian's view of the Geac system not the computer specialist's perspective. I think this is fair since Geac promotes itself as a system for the uninitiated user. Second, note that I am not a Geac salesperson, but, on the other hand, I am not a severe Geac critic either. I suspect, though, that I will seem a little of each. Third, the University of Arizona Library does not have trained computer and systems specialists among its staff. Our current head computer operator is an English major who luckily happened to be employed in the loan department of the university at the time we considered online circulation systems. I say luckily because he (Tom Owens) had worked at Ohio State at the time they were developing their circulation system.

By way of further introduction, I think it will be interesting to note what the University of Arizona asked for (and did not ask for) in its Request for Proposal (RFP) for an online circulation system under the general heading: Management Reports/Notices/Lists. That this request took up most of what was to become page thirteen of the RFP should have given me a clue to our future, both from the standpoint of not asking for the obvious and of asking for the impossible. In quick summary, we wanted:

1. Circulation activity as follows:
   a. patron category,
   b. call number,
   c. classification number,
   d. library,
   e. call number linked to patron category;
2. lists of missing items/replacement items;
3. lists of items that circulate for more than a specified number of times as determined by the library;
4. lists of items that have not circulated in a specified period of time as determined by the library;
5. lists of patrons who are delinquent, owe fines, etc.;
6. overdue search lists;
7. lists of items with more than a specified number of holds or recalls as specified by the library;
8. a daily circulation list on microfiche; and
9. a hold shelf clearance list with cumulative statistical capabilities.

The impossible to secure was circulation information by call number linked to patron category. It was an important piece of information in that we had just gone through the exercise of trying to demonstrate what items faculty and graduate students used in order to comply with U.S. Government standards for the allocation of research overhead. Research overhead to the University of Arizona Library represents a considerable chunk of money each year.

Not asking for the obvious was specifically not requiring that Geac be able to tabulate circulation totals for a given period of time as a standard report. To my amazement, the system still cannot give total circulation counts as a standard report. Why? Because the TSTA Report does not count renewals. Our head computer operator, Tom Owens (who assisted greatly in the preparation of this paper), has written a program to get circulation totals for periods longer than one month (usually for a semester). This report does not count renewals either. The history file must be used to do this. Tom's program requires asking for how many items have circulated more than zero times in a specific location and then cross-multiplying and adding totals for each location in the library system. I tell Tom that he is running the most expensive manual calculator in the history of humankind, but he says research may prove me wrong.

In this discussion we will look at four general areas of the Geac system: what I call circulation management, financial management, the bibliographic and patron extract modules, and finally, system management—how the Geac manages itself. I will begin with circulation.

One of the most often asked questions I hear is: How often did a particular book circulate? Geac provides such information online at the copy level of the bibliographic record. By finding a specific title and then going to the item level screen and keying a copy detail command, one can tell how often a particular item has circulated—up to a maximum of 256 circulations. Libraries having heavy circulation, such as for reserve material, are limited by the 256 count (this will come up again when I talk about reserve circulation). These counts must be zeroed out each semester so that we can obtain accurate reserve circulation counts. Other information available in the online copy detail display is the date the record has last been edited, the date the system was entered, and the number of times an item has been reshelved.

More general, but important, circulation information is available in Geac reports. One of the reports the University of Arizona has been waiting for and just recently received is the Interagency Activity Report. In essence this report gives a general profile of who is using what kind of materials. By defining item material types with some specificity, a library will be able to profile general collection use.

The report is sorted by agency, patron privilege type and material type. Patron privilege type is part of the matrix controlling the loan period. It is more general than patron statistical type which can identify users within narrow categories and is counted in TSTA. Material type is also part of the loan matrix.

In looking at the report, one can see that the privilege type is repeated for each material type on which activity appears, but we plan to change this display to show privilege type only once. Activity can include circulation (charge out) information as well as information on discharges, books placed on reserve (RRP), fines action, holds placed, and partial payments made in the financial module.

The report totals the activity areas within privilege class and material type. It also totals by specific activity and agency. For libraries using departmental codes, such as for academic departments in a college or university, the report also gives total activity. Agency totals are also shown.

After loading departmental codes, we realized that the required manual input of patron data would be too complex and time consuming. We had entered over 100 codes. Thus, all users at the University of Arizona default to one "department." The report cumulates to the point when the file is so large that it needs to be dumped onto tape, for example. The file then zeros out and a new cumulation begins.

One of the things to remember when I discuss various reports is that local policy, database size and long hours of operation can hamper full utilization of some Geac reports. The University of Arizona's Geac database contains over 1.6 million item records represented by approximately 1.2 million titles. There are over 60,000 users in the patron database. Geac's report that lists all of the items' statistics is an example of a report that cannot be successfully run in a large library—at least not at the University of Arizona.

The report produces a list of all item statistics—item being the specific copy of a work. The report is sorted by agency, branch (terminal location), and transaction type. The transactions one might want to report on include charges/discharges, RRPs, fine information, holds, partial payments, or all of these areas.

The sample report from Geac was sorted by charges/discharges. Information reported was the call number, item type, item number, item location, terminal number, transaction date, transaction time, patron number, and patron type. As one can see, for a particular agency and specific date, a wealth of information is available. Finding time to use it all, however, is another matter.

One problem most libraries face is what to do about missing items. The management of missing books has been handled by Geac in two ways:

through the Missing Report and through the utilization of the system's local programming options using a Geac language called GLUG. I want to take a minute and talk about this powerful language with such a funny name.

GLUG is the report-writer language for the Geac system. An interpreted language, it allows the user, even one with moderate sophistication, to create reports, secure in the knowledge that it is almost impossible to make a mistake which would damage the database or affect software support maintenance from Geac. The driver program that interprets the GLUG code has been written so that no data files may be modified by a GLUG program.

Although the language has limitations, it surely would meet the needs of any but the most sophisticated computer operators. GLUG is particularly useful because it can easily overcome the limitations of the bibliographic and patron extract programs which will be presented later.

Staff at the University of Arizona were able to develop useful GLUG programs about two months after the language was made available to us. As an example, our head computer operator has had no formal training in programming and very little experience (as mentioned earlier he somewhat slid into his present position when the system was implemented). He has had no problems developing GLUG programs despite his lack of training. We believe most libraries will find the language easy to use regardless of the level of staffing. Combined with the extract programs, the GLUG language furnishes a package of programs which will allow a library the ability to create many of the reports it needs.

To get back to missing books, the areas in which the University of Arizona needed much help with was good management of what items were missing, no longer missing or still missing at the end of one year. Geac produces, by operator action, a report of missing items. It is sorted by agency, the missing status (there can be a variety of reasons why an item is missing), and by call number. We at Arizona are most interested in the status information. An item listed as missing but subsequently checked out would show as "returned from missing" on this report which modifies the online record to show that the item is no longer missing. The report was particularly useful in the transition from the old missing procedure to the one that is now automated. The zero indication in the status field of the report told us to pull the manual missing card for appropriate action.

Under new procedures, the Bibliographic Extract and a Geac/GLUG program, modified locally by the head computer operator, is used to identify those items missing in the system one year after being declared missing. One of the optional bibliographic fields is used to input the month and year the item is declared missing. One year later the Bibliographic Extract program is run, asking for all books still missing from

March 1981, for example. The report is sorted by call number—which enables staff to search for the material—and is printed by the locally produced program. Those items found are discharged, which "frees" the missing status when the Geac Missing Report is run. The Bibliographic Extract program is then run again, dropping all the discharged items. What remains are those items missing for one year or more. This information is given to the catalog department so that appropriate cards can be withdrawn from the various catalogs, and bibliographic and/or item information deleted from the Geac database.

An additional concern for many libraries, depending upon lending and other policies, is that of the user whose card has expired in the system but who still has material checked out. Geac addresses this management situation through a program that produces a list of all card expired patrons with items checked out.

The report is sorted by agency and then alphabetically by patron name. Patron information provided besides name includes: address, phone number, ID number, and expiry date in the system. Each separate item checked out is listed after the patron information. Thus, if a user had ten items checked out, ten complete patron entries as described earlier would appear. Item information includes call number, author, title, material type, due date, and status other than normal (such as billed for replacement or missing). The report could be useful for a small library which needed to keep track of such information. It could also be useful in any library whose loan policy prevented loan periods to exceed the expiry date. A library could influence when a person showed up on this report (at least in theory) by staggering patron expiry dates in the system.

At the University of Arizona this report is of little use because we *do* allow loan periods to exceed expiry date. One of the reasons we allow this is that library staff could not handle successfully the large end-of-term and/or academic year return or renewal of all materials. Thus, this potentially excellent report is not often run.

It would be unwise to move on to other areas without talking about hold management information and class reserve capabilities. Geac has a variety of report programs dealing with holds. A hold is defined here as that process by which a user can be notified that a specific item has been returned and is waiting on the hold shelf to be picked up.

One of the things called for in the University of Arizona's RFP was a Hold Shelf Clearance Report. My thought was to identify those items which had not been picked up so that they could be pulled from the shelf, and also to keep statistics on the number of such items. (I must tell you that I was alone in wanting such a report. Staff in the hold unit saw little use for it.)

What we received was a report that did list such items, but that also listed holds which had been terminated. (There are at least two ways a hold can be terminated in the system. One way is for it to have been "sitting" for 180 days—waiting to be acted upon when the item is returned. The other is for a staff member to go into the system and terminate the hold.) This list, then, gave us much more than we needed to do the job; so much more that it was far easier to go through the hold shelf manually looking for items that needed to be pulled. However, because the Hold Report was in the GLUG language, we were able to modify it locally without fear of losing software support for the system itself. As a point of information, Geac was unable to provide statistical cumulations in this report.

The report is not useless, it is just that we feel it cannot be used as intended—and I emphasize the *we*. The report could be used in libraries that need more control over, or are interested in, more detailed statistical information about holds. It does give one a good idea of items not picked up and the number of items lapsed in the system. By working with the provided information one could: (1) keep track of which patrons are not picking up holds in order to see if there are notification or other problems in the hold routine; and (2) keep track of the number of holds terminated (not satisfied) by the system.

Three other hold program reports need mentioning. One of these is a report that produces a list of items on which holds have been placed between certain dates determined by the library each time the report is run. Also identified is the patron who requested the hold. It is sorted by the pickup agency and then arranged alphabetically by patron name. When we first looked at this report, we did not quite know how it could be used. Geac, I suspect, like other turnkey vendors, does give descriptions of reports, but does not tell what it might have had in mind in designing the thing. Some reports are rather obvious in their utilization. The Returned From Missing Report needs little context beyond its description.

After talking about this particular report, it did seem that we could have used it if we had so desired. By going into the system and seeing if a recall had also been placed on the item shown, we could, through the timing of the report run, determine what items were not returned by the adjusted recall due date. (It is important to note that one should place a hold on an item when recalling it, although the system will allow a recall without identifying the person needing the material.)

One might think that this report could help measure work load. That is, by running the report daily or weekly, for example, one would know the number of holds placed. This is true, except that the moment a library places terminals for use in public areas and allows users to place holds themselves, the work load utilization is lost. Other libraries may indeed find the report useful, but based upon policy and procedures in place at the University of Arizona, it is not used.

Geac also provides a program which lists the contents of the hold shelf. It is sorted by patron name within pickup agency and lists the patron name, phone number, item information, active and expiry dates. One could also use this list to notify patrons of available material. Arizona does not use this report, but relies instead on the availability notice that is generated when a book with a hold on it is discharged.

The most heavily used holds report at the University of Arizona is the Holds/Purchase Alert Report. It works in part within parameters set by the library in that it allows a library to set the ratio against which the system searches for hits. We use the report to alert us to the possibility of ordering additional copies of high demand material. Currently, three holds against a single copy will trigger inclusion in this report. The bibliographic information is then sent to the acquisitions department for a decision on ordering additional copies.

Since we have just begun to work with this report, it is too early to measure its utility in our particular setting. The report is sorted by location and then by call number. Information displayed includes call number, author and title, location of item, active copies, missing copies, total copies, patron name and phone number, and specific number of the copy on which the hold has been placed. Active copies are those that are displayed when looking at item information, as opposed to copies which have been deleted. Total copies include a running total of all copies that have ever been in the system.

The Data Entry Report, also known at the University of Arizona Library as the infamous accession list, comes in two standard formats: long and short. If one is familiar with the full bibliographic screen in Geac, one gets a good idea of information contained on the long list. If not, it includes: call number, title, author, note, status, entry date, last edit date, copies, accession number, price, barcode number, copy status, copy reference number, user copy number, material type, circulation information, reshelve information, last use date, and all the optional fields. The report is sorted by location and operators' initials. The short form includes call number, title, author, copies, volume, material type, location, date the record was created/updated, and operators' intials.

The Data Entry Report is an excellent source for checking the accuracy of input to the system. In trying to use the short form as an accessions list, however, it fails badly in a number of ways. I mention its use as an accessions list because this is what the Geac system said would fulfill the RFP. Some of the failures are no fault of Geac. We simply do not agree on the definition of accessions which we view as new items not retrospective conversion items. What are the problems with the Data Entry Report? First, the call number field of the report is not large enough to take a long call number. Thus, using the list to identify new material and then to locate the item in a library is often difficult or impossible. Second, the author and title fields are often not large enough to display sufficient information. The field sizes might also be an argument against this intended use, except that we believe the full report does give complete information.

The real problem in using the short form as an accessions list is that it shows every record entered into the system from any source. Thus, it is much more than a new accessions list. Hence the name: Data Entry Report. It is so logical when one thinks about it, but it surely doesn't work for us.

We have reworked the report through a locally written program to eliminate extraneous information and expand the call number field so that a full number is displayed. This can all be done without altering the Geac software supporting the standard report. To get around the too much information problem, we are working on a program that will hit against a combination of OCLC number or one other hook such as LCCN or ISSN numbers. Our head catalog librarian feels that the retrospective input now being done in branch collections will not often have an OCLC number, but may have other hooks. All data being entered through the OCLC/Geac Link, which was developed by our head catalog librarian working with Geac systems staff, contains the OCLC number and other identifiers such as LCCN and ISSN numbers. In this way we hope to refine output to reflect better new accessions. While on the one hand we would have wished an easier way to get at new accessions, on the other we are thankful for the flexibility of the Geac system to allow local GLUG programming.

In an academic setting, class reserves are an important component of a circulation department. One of the strong points of the Geac program when we were looking at circulation systems was its reserve system. I want to talk about two reserve-connected reports: the Weeding and Stamping List and the Reserve Use Report.

The Weeding and Stamping List is not used at the University of Arizona, but it is an interesting report. To our knowledge it was developed at the request of another Geac library which handles class reserves differently from many libraries we are familiar with. When a reserve list is entered into the system, the online operator indicates when the items are to go on reserve. This program identifies those items in the Geac database which are to go on class reserve between specified dates. After the program is run, the items are displayed automatically in the system as being on reserve with the appropriate reduced loan periods and reserve fine rules in place. The list can be printed to allow staff either to pull material to place in a special reserve location or to use as a listing of what is currently on reserve. From the perspective of listing and automatic display of reserve status, the program is a powerful one.

However, because we place reserve material in reserve book rooms, we are reluctant to use this program for fear that there will not be sufficient human resources to pull identified material from the stacks in a timely enough manner before it shows on reserve. We prefer to pull the material first and then place them on reserve, using other Geac reserve functions.

The Weeding and Stamping List is sorted by call number, and lists typical bibliographic information such as author, title and item number. Also shown is the course name, active date and expiry date. Similarly the program will automatically remove material from reserve when the expiry date is reached.

Another component of management information for class reserve is Geac's program that produces the reserve use report. The standard report is sorted by course and then by professor's name. As one can see, the course is listed only once with the professor's name directly under. Bibliographic information is listed by material type within professor's name, and then by call number, author and title. This is followed by the item barcode number for each item, the item location (this could be different from item to item if a library did not have a centralized reserve room), material type, circulation count, and reshelve count. Through local programming, other sorts are possible such as a call number within a course.

As designed, the report is useful in giving professors information on what items placed on class reserve are used, and in many cases not used at all. Most of us know that the information will have little impact in putting together next year's class reserve list. We view this report as we do filling out income tax forms. The process probably would not go far in helping us, but we are surely damned if it is not filled out and mailed on time.

A major problem with the concept of this report is that one cannot delete material from reserve before running it. In doing so, the circulation counts for the reserve status are lost. It is not that the count disappears, but simply that since (presumably) the item is back in the regular stack location, the circulation information will only show as general circulation. Another real problem with the report, as we understand the system, is that circulation counts stop when 256 circulations are reached. We know that many photocopied items circulate more than this amount. Thus, circulation counts for reserve courses are not necessarily accurate.

Before moving into the financial areas of the Geac system, I want to talk a bit about the TSTA Report I mentioned very early in this paper. At first glance one might think that this reports total circulation counts and other statistics by hour of day. But, as I said earlier, it is not so! The value of this report is not to be found in its ability to count circulation, because renewals are not counted by any standard Geac program.

What is valuable is that one can tell circulation (minus renewals), discharges, RRPs, fine activity, and holds placed by hour of the day for each location defined within the system. Currently at the University of Arizona, statistics are shown for the Science-Engineering Library, the Main Library, Government Documents Department, the Library Science Library, the music collection, the Arizona Health Sciences Center Library (which is sharing the system with us) and for the two major reserve book room operations in the main and science-engineering libraries. The report totals each activity by hour and by the day, as well as cross tabulating each activity by location. All totals cumulate monthly when a new count begins. If this report counted renewal activity, it would give a complete picture of major circulation activity for each hour of every day the library was open. Currently, the value of this report is in demonstrating first-time circulation and other activities that are useful in planning desk coverage (for example, the assumption that renewal activity parallels circulation activity). A program is being devised to add all of these figures and graph the results by hour.

A separate area of this report gives the same activity breakdowns by patron statistical class. Remember, statistical class can define a narrow category of users. For example, by looking at the report for 14 April 1982, one can see that UAFRESH (University of Arizona freshmen) checked out 7675 items system-wide, returned 6205 items system-wide, had 145 fines issued and placed 128 hold requests for a total month-to-date activity of 14,155. The latter figure is a mixture of "apples and oranges," but it does give one a figure to compare with other statistical classes to demonstrate library use or at least circulation-related use. Except for not counting renewals—a gross omission—it is a very good report.

Before entering the turnkey circulation marketplace, Geac was heavily involved in banking systems, and still is. I say this because we are now entering into that portion of Geac's circulation system which deals with fines, bills for replacement and the like. Very detailed information is provided online for each user having a fine or replacement bill, including the ability to manually or automatically block usage of the system by a patron when financial obligations reach certain levels. Although strong in the main, the program does have quirks—at least as perceived by the staff at Arizona.

First, one has the ability to modify a billed amount downward, but there is no corresponding ability to modify it upward. As a matter of policy, all bills for replacement are issued at $35 per item. However, if a patron challenges this amount, the fines office staff will seek a price for the item with the understanding that if it is more that $35, the higher amount will be billed. To do so, and it is done very infrequently, is difficult. Either one has to discharge the item in question then manually input "fake" charge-out-and-return information and then input the price, or one can add on the higher amount in the processing fee field.

Second, in calculating the amount owed to stop (block) users from the system, Geac as standard policy counts only fines—not bills for replacement. I mention this to give you some idea of areas in which online turnkey reality differs from local reality. The financial programs, though, both operationally and report-wise, are essentially good.

One of the benefits the University of Arizona was looking for from an online system was an interface between the system billing a user for replacement of a long overdue item and somehow notifying the fines office staff that the particular item had been returned *if* payment had already been received for the item. Such an interface is available in the report titled LBPATE. This program produces a list of all patrons who are eligible for refunds. It is a report we have not often used, but will do so in the future. The report can be sorted by item barcode number and by patron name. Both are valuable. The information contained in the program includes patron ID number, patron name, return date, item barcode number, and amount of refund.

One may think that such a report as LBPATE is not necessary. I say this because that was told to me by certain loan staff. The theme went something like this: No one who has paid for a book and then returns it will let the matter drop without coming in and demanding (not asking, mind you) for a refund. Not so! I am saying that some of our assumptions about how users act or react are not necessarily true. There are certain kinds of users who do not come into the library and inquire about refunds. However, the LBPATE report also serves another purpose. It provides the library the opportunity to make a refund when a book paid for by a patron simply shows up. While I do not like to admit it—especially for publication—I guess we do make mistakes from time to time, and both staff and patron do not discharge material correctly or manage to shelve it in the wrong place. This report gives us an opportunity to refund a fine when the error has been ours. We like this report very much!

When a library collects money and/or modifies fines, financial management information is of paramount importance. The Geac system does some interesting things in this area, not all of which work in a library setting such as at the University of Arizona. There is excellent online information by patron query and by bibliographic query on fines, missing status, and billing for replacement items. For example, if I were billed for the late return of the book *Old Man and the Sea*, the information would show on the Bibliography Query and also on my patron record. However, the minute I pay the fine things become a bit confusing. I say this because staff in the library fines office often have to refer back to the Geac-produced Fines Journal to document payment or other action. The journal is pro-

duced as part of overnight processing. It lists all activity of the financial
module for the previous day and shows, for example, payments, modifica-
tions, cancellations, and refunds. The problem—and it is a big one—is that
information is sorted (printed) by time of day. Thus, if I paid a bill two
weeks ago, but didn't quite know when or what day, the staff might have to
look through all Fines Journals scanning each day for my name.

To overcome nervous breakdowns by fines office staff and to protect
me from attack, our head computer operator asked Geac to report the
information by patron name. One still has to look through daily journals,
but it is much easier with a name sort than the time of day sort provided by
the standard report program.

One of the nonstandard reports that we occasionally use is the printing of financial records for a single user. Again, we have written a GLUG
program which will print all financial obligations for a library patron.
This is useful when dealing with users who have a lengthy record and who
want a hard copy with which to work. The report information is in no
particular order, but it does include call number, title, author, item
number, charge out, and due date information as well as returned date and
time as applicable, and fine amount for each item returned late. The
GLUG program also prints out a list of what material a person has checked
out. We do not advertise these reports, but rather refer users to a public
query terminal to look up their own records. I want to emphasize again
that there are many reports that can be "programmed" locally without the
services of a formally trained computer operator. I will discuss this in
greater detail in the section on Bibliographic and Patron Extract modules.

One of the things we did not do well (in fact we didn't do it at all) was
to specify in our RFP that the Geac system have a program to transfer
financial information from the system to the university business office. I
mention this to point out that one cannot assume a vendor will provide
what may seem obvious.

The University of Arizona has a policy of collecting fines in the
library. However, according to state law all fine amounts must be transferred to the business office so that student records can be encumbered.
Geac does have a program to do this, but in our opinion it is so tailored to a
specific Geac site that it is of no use to us at all. The Geac-developed
program dumps aggregate financial information onto the tape for transfer
to a business office. In doing so, however, all library financial online
records are wiped clean. This was unacceptable to the University of Arizona Library because we are more interested in getting material back through
talking with users than we are in collecting money. We are now working
with the Geac system and the university's business office to develop a taped
snapshot of student financial records to transfer into the university's
encumbrance system while still retaining financial information in the

Geac database. It is important to note that this capability is above the cost of the initial system.

The Geac does provide the capability to print out total financial records. In fact the library was asked to run this report in lieu of having a tape transfer program in place. We did this with humorous results—at least from our point of view. After an hour or so, we were able to begin printing. When we were 1 percent of the way through printing, we had a 40-page output and the operator made a few quick calculations. Determining that he would be there ten hours, he terminated the program. Clearly the report was possible to produce, but our estimates were that the business office would have a pile of paper over three feet high. Upon notification of this reality, they decided to overlook the fact that student library fines would once again not be part of the encumbrance system.

This report, like some others that Geac provides, can be run more reasonably in a small institution with small patron (bibliographic) databases. It would certainly be difficult to run such a report in a library the size of the University of Arizona's.

The report, I think, would work very well with the standard transfer program Geac has developed as part of the turnkey system. A library could run the patron financial report prior to running the transfer program. In doing so, staff would have a record of patron financial information, although it would mean going through each report to locate a specific patron record.

The last report I want to discuss in the financial area is Geac's standard Long Overdue Summary Report. It lists items overdue beyond a time period defined by the library. The report is sorted by call number and displays the patron name, item number, call number/author/title, due date, return date, fine amount, price, and type. The report has as its main use, we think, that of searching for overdue material. It is another report that is of little utility to the University of Arizona for a number of reasons which may not apply to other libraries. Once again our size and policy/procedures are against us. The report is cumulative and reports all items fitting the time frame profile. The potential problem with this report, as we understand it, is that over time it would become too large for a limited staff to use for searching or even notifying users in an attempt to retrieve material. Currently at the University of Arizona, there are over 1200 items represented on this report.

I would like now to discuss that portion of the Geac system with which I personally have the least familiarity because the programs are executed by computer operators only—Bibliographic and Patron Extracts. The Bibliographic Extract is a statistical tool which allows one to design reports for most bibliographic entries in the system. When looking at it, it is probably more important to explain what cannot be done rather than what can be accomplished. Outstanding limitations of the system include: (1) bibliographic entries that do not have copy level information cannot be accessed; (2) current transaction data is not accessible, and historical transaction data is limited; and (3) the circulation counter does not count renewals. The operator can define rules using fields either at the copy (item) level of a record or at the bibliographic level (data relevant to all copies of the title). One may decide to either count the number of matches for the rules defined or else to print a list of all items that matched the rules. Geac does not sort the data to be printed, but the sort can be easily arranged.

Although, in theory, the Bibliographic Extract can combine almost any number of rules in any combination of item and title level information, we have found that, in reality, certain requests cause the program to run so slowly that it is greatly reduced in effectiveness. As an example, it runs particularly slow when asked to look for certain call number ranges— e.g., all call numbers beginning with QA. Although we had hoped to use the extract program to count collection growth, such programs take too long to run. We can ask for the number of books in a particular agency which have circulated more than N times, but we cannot ask for books that have circulated to a specific patron class more than N times, because this information is not stored in files the extract can access. We can also ask for a list of books in a specific location which have not circulated since a specified date, but may not ask for a list of books currently charged out. Despite its limitations, we find the Bibliographic Extract to be extremely useful. Data which may be defined includes, but is not limited to, the following:

At the bibliographic level, deleted titles, titles which are part of a multi-volume set, data-verified titles, reordered titles, titles added online, titles with notes, titles bound with other titles, number of pending holds on a title, call number/author/title of a work, notes added to a bibliographic record, publisher of a title, subject of a title, system accession number, date the record was created, date of last update, ISBN number, LC card number, library-defined optional fields (8), OCLC number, local accession number, the price of a book, and the number of copies.

At the item level, the data which may be defined includes the material type, whether an item is missing and the missing type, the item's normal location, whether a copy has been deleted, whether a copy belongs to the library, whether a book is missing, whether an item is on reserve and reserve type, copy is bound with, whether it is fine type, the number of times the copy was charged out, number of times copy was discharged when not previously charged, copy barcode number, transaction indicator, system reference number, date of last change, local copy specific call number, local copy number, secondary location, and library defined optional fields (4).

The Patron Extract works much like the Bibliographic Extract, with many of the same virtues and limitations. One may define a number of rules, then either list or count the number of patrons who match those rules. The Patron Extract gives more access to the transaction file, but does not allow one to print any specific items charged to any specific patron. Because reserve courses are actually pseudo-borrowers, the Patron Extract also allows some access to the reserve subsystem. Information which may be defined includes, but is not limited to, the following:

the borrower's ID number;
whether the borrower's privileges have been suspended and a notice sent;
whether the borrower has recalled books and a notice has been sent;
whether the borrower has been sent an overdue notice;
if the borrower has overdue books;
whether the borrower has an informative message in his record;
if the borrower has an incomplete address (determined by the library);
if the borrower has satisfied lapsed or terminated holds;
whether a borrower's badge has been reported lost, missing or stolen.

An expanded list is included as an appendix to this paper. The last area of management that will be discussed are the Geac system's management capabilities.

Geac takes care of itself very well; in some ways better than it does those of us who seek more from it than it can supply. Geac provides excellent system management information which is generated in the overnight processing routines. These routines are done most nights at the University of Arizona. Very briefly I want to discuss some of the information contained in these reports, all of which to me have very strange names.

One of the most carefully watched reports is LPFCHK which, among other things, tells us the growth of various files in the system. I frequently watch the percent column of the report which states how full each file is. Major files contained in this report include text, history, item, transaction, patron, and interagency. The computer operators not only are concerned with how full files are, but the rate of a file's growth. We pay particular attention to the history file because it tends to overflow rather easily.

The TSTA report has been discussed previously. I mention it here only to point out again that it is generated in overnight processing and could be considered a systems management report. The Terminal Line Analysis Report is one that only a computer nut or a very statistically minded librarian would enjoy. It is Geac's way of telling us how hard it has worked any given day. The important information contained in this report falls into two areas: port activity and terminal activity. Each port in the system is listed with the number of sends (each time someone hits the send key and a command goes to the computer) and the total number of characters (the nonhuman kind) represented by the sends, which are also known as GODO counts. The first portion of this report totals the number of sends and the number of characters sent. Looking further, one can find out how active each specific terminal was for the day in question by looking at the terminal detail portion of the report. Contained here is the terminal number, the number of sends for the terminal, the number of characters represented, the number of wands represented (my favorite statistic), the number of wand errors (most always zero), and the number of times the terminal had to be reset. I exaggerate somewhat when I make fun of this information, for what one has here is the ability to monitor terminal use. For example, by knowing where terminal number ten is located, one is able to see (perhaps) that it is not getting much use and should be moved elsewhere. The decision is always being made, of course, by someone other than I. As a matter of possible interest, we find that public query terminals get the most use.

The reset statistics prove valuable in two related instances: when the University of Arizona first came online and also as we brought new sites onto the system. One most often has to reset (cancel out a screen display and bring back the general menu) when one does not know what to do next. By watching reset activity, loan department training staff were able to zero in on potential problem sites. Of course we did not know what the problem was, but we could pretty well be sure one was present. In addition, this report is essential to the recovery process should the system have a fatal shutdown.

LPOVR is a rather cumbersome report which, among other things, gives the total borrower records, item records, and call number records in the database. This report also displays summary details of notices sent. However, this is not to be confused with individual pieces of paper processed (in our case, stuffed into envelopes), but rather totals for the different kinds of notices generated. We, like many libraries with Geac systems, use a multipurpose form on which a variety of different kinds of notices can be found—e.g., on the same piece of paper can appear an overdue fine, a recall and first overdue date.

Areas covered statistically for notices generated include totals for number of records output (the total of various kinds of notices); bills for replacement created; processing fees created; the number of first, second and third overdues; fines; recalls placed including reserve recalls; available notices; cancelled holds; expired holds; number of term notices sent (at Arizona this represents faculty and staff reminder notices); processing fees; replacement bills; number of items sent for collection; and finally, the number of long-overdues generated. Other useful information provided by the LPOVR Report is the total dollar amount of overdue fines payable, the total of fines owed (overdue but not yet returned, thus the fine is not yet totaled), and the total overdue fines and fines owed. By using this report, one is able to get a general idea of notice and financial activity for the day in question. Early on, I spent each morning going through all the overnight processing reports.

One report that is very useful, particularly with regard to having the Geac comply with response time mandates in our contract, is a report that lists terminal response times. It is a complicated report to understand, but Tom Owens tells me Geac personnel have been very patient in their explanations. We look at this report daily for signs of response problems.

The final Geac looks-at-itself report I want to present is one that gives what I call demographic statistical information. Displayed are the number of transactions and borrower records on file as well as transaction counts for the following: charges, discharges, fines (lumped together); holds; RRPs; financial; partial payments; current books on loan; current books on term loan; current books on reserve; and missing books on loan. Other information presented may be of interest to a computer operator, but has little value to me. Included are such things as data on the longest transaction chain, number of financial chains, and so on.

We have now completed looking at the four areas of management information one can obtain from the Geac system: circulation, financial, bibliographic and patron extract, and how the system manages itself. If I had time this afternoon to make two points only, they would be that there may not be such an animal as turnkey reality, just different local realities that have needs which may or may not be met with a system called "turnkey"; and always ask for the obvious and then always expect the unexpected when dealing with the turnkey marketplace.

APPENDIX

Data Elements for the Bibliographic
and Patron Extract Module Programs

In Bibliographic Extract Module programs, data which may be defined include the following categories:

At the Bibliographic Level:
    deleted titles
    titles part of a multi-volume set
    data verified titles
    reordered titles
    titles added online
    titles with notes
    number of pending holds on a title
    call number, author and title of an item
    notes added to a bibliographic record
    publisher of a title (when data available)
    subject of a title (when data available)
    system accession number
    date record was created
    date of last update
    ISBN number
    LC card number
    library defined optional fields (eight available)
    OCLC number
    local accession number
    price of book
    number of copies

At the Item Level:
    material type
    item is missing and missing type
    item in normal location
    copy has been deleted (CPY*DEL)
    book is missing
    item is on reserve and reserve type
    copy is a bound with
    copy has fine type
    number of times copy was charged
    number of times copy was discharged when not previously charged
    copy barcode number
    transaction indicator
    system reference number
    date of last charge
    local (copy specific) call number
    local copy number
    secondary location
    library defined optional fields (four available)

Boolean strategies within these categories can also consider the reverse meanings as well (e.g., listing all items with three or more pending holds but without a note added to the bibliographic record, if so desired).

In Patron Extract Module programs, similar boolean strategies can be programmed. Information which can be accessed by the Patron Extract includes (but is not limited to):

borrower's ID number
borrower's privileges have been suspended and a notice sent
borrower has recalled books and a notice has been sent
borrower has overdue books
borrower has been sent an overdue notice
borrower has an informative message in his record
borrower has an incomplete address (as determined by the library)
borrower has satisfied, lapsed or terminated holds
borrower's badge has been reported lost, missing or stolen
borrower has an overdue recalled book
borrower's privileges have been stopped because a book is too long overdue
borrower's fines are over the limit set by the library
borrower's privilege class
borrower's record was created online
borrower has transactions
borrower surname
borrower initials
borrower note text
number of books a borrower has on loan
number of books a borrower has been billed for
number of reserve loans for a borrower
both borrower's home and local address
borrower's phone number
borrower's statistical class
date borrower was registered
date borrower's current validation expires
borrower's barcode number
library defined optional fields (six available)
borrower's agency
reserve borrower's course name
reserve borrower's professor's name
number of borrower's current and/or deleted transactions
number of CDFs (charges, discharges, fine transactions) for the borrower
number of items on reserve for reserve patrons
number of financial transactions for the borrower
number of hold transactions for the borrower
number of partial payments of fines the borrower currently has
number of unpaid fines the borrower has
number of fines the borrower has which have relevant correspondence
number of inactive fines a borrower has
number of fines available for refund for a borrower
number of overdue fines for the borrower
number of recalls for the borrower
number of processing fees accessed by the library
number of refunds the library has given the patron (For example, the Patron
 Extract system can tell us how many patrons have more than twenty unpaid
 fines, but not how many patrons owe more than $30.)

JOHN N. OLSGAARD

Graduate Student
Graduate School of Library and Information Science
University of Illinois at Urbana-Champaign

Characteristics of Managerial Resistance to Library Management Information Systems

Most of the presentations given at this clinic have made two assumptions: that library managers understand the functioning and capabilities of automated systems; and, given that they understand the system, that they will utilize the information generated by these systems. These may not always be valid assumptions. To illustrate this fact, several years ago I was asked to be a member of a library systems study team. As part of my duties during the course of that study, I analyzed the patterns of questions that had been asked hourly at the main reference desk for the previous years. After considerably torturing the data, I developed a prediction model that was intended to serve as a guide for adequately staffing the reference desk at any particular time. The lengthy report I submitted contained graphs, tables and explanations of the entire process. The pride of this report was a day-by-day weighted listing of reference activity gauged by the time of the academic year. About three weeks after I submitted this portion of the study to the library director, he asked me to come back for a conference. As I walked into his office, he had my three foot long day-by-day graph layed out on the table, studying it intently. The director was repeatedly saying, "Beautiful, just beautiful." Then he looked up at me, smiled, and said, "But what does it mean?" After attempting to explain the significance of the report, I had the feeling that he still thought it looked pretty, but had no real meaning.

The point of this story is that management information systems are worthless if the manager either does not understand the information, or refuses to use the information. This is particularly relevant since for the past decade libraries have shown a determined interest in the prospects of automating various clerical processes. Only recently has this interest begun to include management processes as being applicable to library automation. In a recent issue of *College & Research Libraries,* Robert S. Runyon suggested that library management is now ripe for automated administrative information gathering systems.[1]

Runyon is no doubt correct in his belief that the library management profession will be examining the concept of management information systems (MIS) more closely in the future. However, his thinking is based on the assumption that library managers will use the systems once they are available. This paper is founded on the premise that in most libraries the current information that is derived from automated systems is a nonutilized or underutilized commodity in the management process. The purpose of this study is to examine the characteristics of this failure to use management information. This examination will consist of three major sections:

1. An examination of how the library as an organization has been responding to a changing environment, both externally and internally.
2. An investigation of the causes of the nonuse of information derived from automated systems in the decision-making process.
3. An analysis of the rationale for using this kind of information in the management process.

Organizational Reaction to External and Internal Stimuli

Most libraries have a problem keeping their clients totally satisfied with the service their organization provides. One almost comes to expect the regular grilling in the newspapers over what the libraries are, or are not, doing to our unsuspecting public. Further, the litany of internal employee problems has become as common as news of another budget cut. The library in today's environment faces what those in management circles might call a marketing problem.

Most marketing problems are really exchange problems. A diagram of the exchange process is given in figure 1. For example, if you go to eat in a university cafeteria the obvious exchange would be the cost of less personalized service and uncomfortable seating for the benefits of fast service and no tipping.

External Stimuli

On the external exchange level, organizations can be seen, in a naturalistic sense, as having a symbiotic relationship with the community they serve. Each element—the organization and the community—have a mutually beneficial effect. The organization provides a service needed by the community, and in return the community supports the organization. The

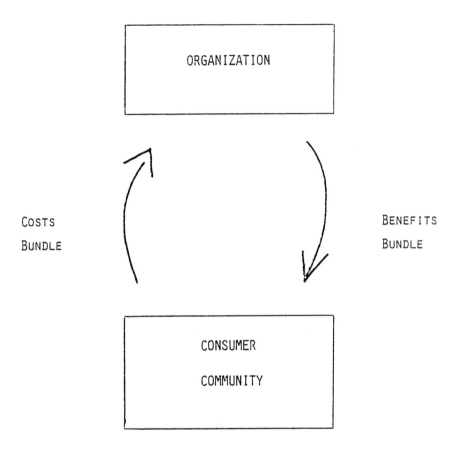

Fig. 1. Representation of the Exchange Process in Marketing

problem is that this relationship is not static. As the environment changes, both the community and organizational needs change. When the service needs of the community either out pace the ability of the organization, or when the service needs of the community cannot be fulfilled by the organization, we perceive what Miriam A. Drake has termed *performance gaps.*[2]

The first symptom of a performance gap is an organizational version of stress. Miller has suggested that stress occurs in an individual when either there is a lack of some essential input, or when an excess of input floods the system.[3] Meier has taken this concept a step further by suggesting that the same kind of stress experienced by individuals can affect organizations. Meier postulates that as the imbalances that occur between the demand for an organization's services and that organization's ability to deliver those services increases, the amount of stress on the organization will increase.[4] As the imbalance grows more severe, the organization experiences the equivalent of a nervous breakdown. The organization simply stops functioning. This phenomenon is illustrated in figure 2.

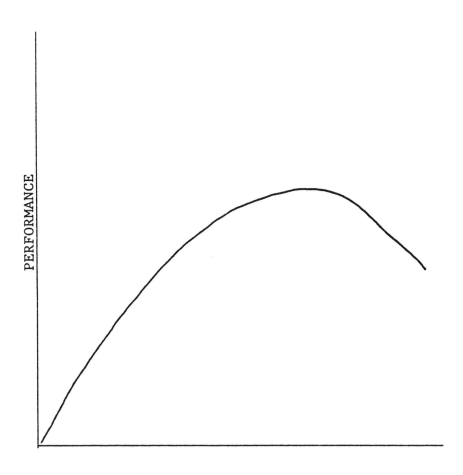

DEMAND

Fig. 2. Example of the Affects of Stress on an Organization as Demand Increases (Modified from Meier, Richard L. "Information Input Overload: Features of Growth in Communications-Oriented Institutions. In *Mathematical Explorations in Behavioral Science,* edited by Fred Massarik and Philburn Ratoosh, p. 268. Homewood, Ill.: Dorsey Press, 1965.)

For example, those of you who are familiar with academic libraries may recognize this kind of deterioration occurring during the weeks preceding final examinations. As the demand for services of the academic library increases, it is met with increased performance from the library's staff. However, the situation reaches the point where the staff is performing at its maximum level while the demand for service continues to increase. This is typified by overcrowded study areas and long lines at the circulation and reference desk. The staff quickly discovers that no matter how hard or how fast they work, their efforts will not keep up with demand. It is at this point that the organization gives up trying to keep pace with demand; the staff either sets its own performance pace regardless of the demand, or begins a policy of high absenteeism in an attempt to ignore the demand.

It is the library manager's job to ensure that this kind of breakdown does not happen in a library organization. When a performance gap begins to occur between the library and its community, the library manager must either seek a new community or alter the library to provide new services. The essential problems that the library manager must solve are: (1) to recognize that an imbalance or performance gap exists, and (2) to know what direction the organization should move to correct the imbalance. It can be suggested that the past performance record of library managers in solving these kinds of problems has been something less than totally successful.

Roger Horn has suggested that this poor performance record for libraries is attributable to what he believes to be the generally poor quality of administrators libraries attract.[5] Without disclaiming that there are poor library managers in the field, or that they have committed some truly magnificent decisional blunders, one hopes that there are other reasons for this failure—other than lack of talent.

Internal Stimuli

Many library managers and automation specialists believe that since they do not have much contact with the general public, this exchange process really does not apply. However, in a similar way, the exchange process occurs every day within the organization. For automation specialists, the primary consumers are probably library managers; for library managers the direct consumers of their product (i.e., administrative decisions) are other librarians within their organization. The basis of the exchange for library managers are fair administrative decisions in return for organizational power and, presumably, loyalty from their employees. These intraorganizational exchanges are as important as the exchange between the organization and the ultimate user community. It could further be submitted that there has been a history of unnecessarily limited cooperation in these intraorganizational exchanges. Automation specialists and library managers, as respective groups, have based their products on an internally-oriented viewpoint. That is, these respective groups have been so interested in the manner, the form and the process of how their products are generated that they tend to forget how the products are utilized.

Alan R. Andreasen has devised a checklist of "yes or no" questions to determine if an individual's or institution's service is too internally oriented:

1. Is customer ignorance *the* barrier to the success of your product? In other words, if people weren't so stupid, they would see the importance of your service.
2. Is your product inherently good?
3. Do you view the consumer as "the enemy?" If the people who use your service would just leave you alone everything would be perfect.
4. Do you see your marketing problem as changing consumer rather than changing the product?
5. Is communication the only really important marketing tool needed to push your product?
6. Do you believe consumer research isn't really necessary?
7. Do you believe consumers of your product are all the same?[6]

If the answer is "yes" to all or most of these questions, the institution's service is too internally oriented, and probably most librarians and libraries suffer from this malady. On the one hand the automation specialists are justifiably proud of the kind of timely information services they can provide, but consider themselves hindered by the library managers that use their product because the managers seem incapable of understanding the most basic data computations. On the other hand are the library managers who view the automation specialists as some kind of vague reincarnation of Dr. Strangelove—those who relate well to their machines, but have little grasp of the real world.

What has occurred in the case of library managers and information specialists is a failure on the part of both parties to properly understand the exchange process involved. Similarly, the automation specialist wants the benefits (i.e., a job and good facilities), without attempting to understand the kinds of services or costs that will be required. What others have called a "breakdown in communications" is what Meltzer claims is actually a loss of information.[7]

This internal information exchange can perhaps be best explained by use of diagrams (see figs. 3 and 4). In figure 3 one can see the familiar pattern of a typical organizational chart. However, a better way to view the communication between the various administrative levels can be seen in

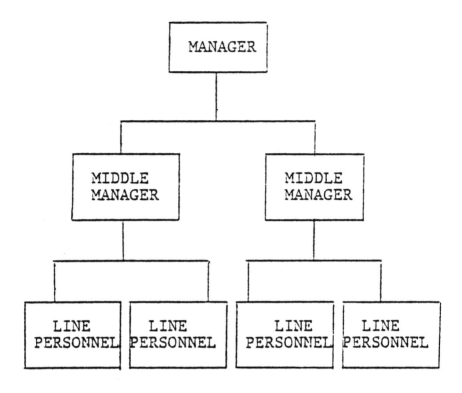

CLIENT COMMUNITY

Fig. 3. Example of a Typical Organization Structure

figure 4. The manager only has direct communication with the middle managers, the middle managers directly communicate with line personnel, and line personnel with the clients. The manager has knowledge of what clients are interested in or what problems they are experiencing only as that information is filtered through the organization's line personnel, and refiltered through middle management. Concomitantly, an adminis-

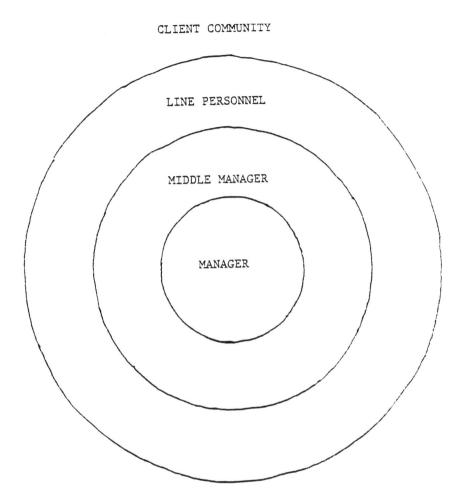

Fig. 4. Representation of Communication Between Organization Levels

trative decision to change the direction of the organization goes through somewhat the same filtering process as it progresses outward from the manager; the decision at each level is filtered, interpreted and readjusted.

This situation is rather common; at each level the basic information is reformulated in terms of the individual desires and political considerations at that level. At each additional level the person who needs to make the decision only has the word of the people at the earlier level that the situation they are describing is accurate. For instance, the people at the manager or middle manager level have become desensitized to increased budget requests because that tends to be the only kind of information they receive. Managers have found that there are very few instances where employees claim that they have too much of anything or wish to have something cut from their budget.

The basic problem with this loss of administrative information between the various organizational levels is that the decision-makers in the library have no reliable benchmark with which to gauge the importance of the request. As such, libraries rarely make informed organizational decisions to meet the needs of their clients or employees. The library must be able to legitimately view itself as a dynamic entity that can successfully react to its changing environment.

The internal exchange failure within a library can exacerbate an external exchange imbalance. For instance, if the public services staff reports to the library manager that demand for a certain subject is outstripping the collection, the library manager must decide if the information is accurate enough to warrant a change of policy. This is where information derived from automated systems could play a major role. Most automated circulation systems can generate a frequency list of circulated materials. In addition, many automated acquisition systems can produce similar frequency lists. Thereby, the library manager can use the circulation information as a benchmark of the demand for a certain subject, and the acquisition information as a gauge of how well the library is responding to the demand. The library manager can then make a rational decision on whether the demand requires an additional appropriation.

In many libraries these automated systems already exist, and in most cases a byproduct of the systems include the above mentioned report features. Unfortunately, library managers for the most part have refused to incorporate these channels into their decision-making plan. Understanding the causes of nonuse of information derived from automated systems constitutes a major dilemma for library organizations.

Causes of Nonuse of Information Derived from
Automated Systems in the Decision-Making Process

The general causes of managerial resistance to information derived from automated systems can be loosely grouped into four categories: (1) educational deficiencies, (2) sensory and decisional deficiencies, (3) cultural deficiencies, and (4) the "priesthood effect."

Educational Deficiencies
Much of the blame for the failure of library managers to utilize automated data has been attributed to the inability of managers to understand the largely numerical-based format of the data, and admittedly, the

inability of software manufacturers to create formats that make this kind of data easier to understand. Shera has suggested that a sixth year of study be added to library science programs to make up for these educational deficiencies.[8] Divilbiss goes one step further to recommend the recruitment of undergraduate science majors into the profession. He points out that many librarians not only have little previous academic training in fields that lend themselves to fully understand automated systems, but generally receive little help in this area when they reach library school.[9] This generalization can perhaps be expected. After all, librarians are either directly involved with, or are the product of, the educational process. As such we tend to view solutions to many problems in an educational light.

Although the educational deficiencies of librarians certainly have a part to play in the nonuse of data derived from automated systems, it is probably too glib to rest the entire explanation on this factor. A strictly educational causation would lend itself to a relatively simple solution— get the necessary education through a course or two in statistics and computer science.

One of the foundations of this paper is to suggest that several other factors may be operant in any given situation, but not that all are occurring at the same time or in equal amounts.

Sensory and Decisional Deficiencies
The first of these factors has to do with information overload. The automated systems that library managers are—or will be—dealing with have reached a level of sophistication that they can generate mountains of data at the touch of a button. The problem comes from trying to interpret all of this information in a rational, logical manner. This may be a classic case of what Toffler referred to in *Future Shock*.[10] There are many examples of where individuals who are faced with increasingly difficult decisional tasks will give up attempting to cope with the new stimuli. They simply quit trying to process the new information. The ability of automated systems to generate data has far outreached the library manager's ability to interpret that information and react to it in a useful way.

David Firnberg has pointed out that when faced with a frustration, like information overload, we react as any animal would when confronted with an obstacle: "the animal either lies down pretending not to notice and goes to sleep; or it rejects the situation, turns its back and walks away; or it battles and tries to master and overcome the cause of its frustration. In our reactions most of us fall into the first two categories."[11] Unfortunately it is rather easy for information overload to occur. Both Posner and Miller have demonstrated the rather severe cognitive limitations of the human mind.[12]

It could be argued that this is merely an extension of the argument that the solution rests in better educational training (i.e., the better the education, the better the individual will cope with the information). Melnyk has suggested that those who have been instructed in the use of a computer facility will experience less frustration than those with no training.[13] This would no doubt help. However, it can be suggested that the capacity of such systems would quickly outreach even the highly trained individual.

Cultural Deficiencies

One of the less talked about reasons for managers not using data derived from automated systems are various inherited cultural biases. One of these biases would include a basic resistance to machines of any kind, particularly machines whose functioning is difficult to understand. One remembers that during the industrial revolution in England some of the workers, the Luddites, destroyed looms. More recent examples would include the numerous instances of people punching extra holes in computer billing cards, or the individuals who input obscene entries into a national cataloging database. In fact, one of the major papers given at the 1981 ACRL National Conference was presented by Paul Lacey and was entitled "Views of a Luddite."[14] It would probably be safe to say that the computer inspires as much distrust as any other technological innovation of our day.

This kind of resistance as demonstrated by managers has been the subject of a number of studies. Ennis has explored the resistance of librarians to automation.[15] Others have attempted to identify the characteristics of those managers that are prone to resist automation efforts. A recent *Business Week* reported the results of a survey conducted by Booz, Allen and Hamilton, Inc. on this topic.[16] It was found that older managers who had been with the same company for a long time tended to be far more resistant than younger executives who had moved from one company to another.

It is interesting to note that this is the same result postulated by Rose in 1969. Rose theorized that older managers who had a long tenure with the same company tended to be more resistant because their strength and organizational power stemmed from a superior knowledge of the current system. Since automation would disrupt that system, it posed a threat to the older executive.[17]

De Greene has suggested that resistance to automation is not unique to the personal characteristics of managers, but it is unique how automation affects their particular positions within the organization.[18] Managers who were favorably disposed toward automation when it meant the elimination of clerical employees, are now suddenly very resistant when managerial-level positions may be eliminated.

Aside from the the fear factor of automation, even intelligent people have a basic distrust of computer-generated data. They have a feeling that somehow the machine has made a mistake. Thereby any decisions they would make on the basis of that data would be faulty. There are scientists who will run their calculations on the computer, and then cross-check them on their calculators just to be sure. They know that the odds against the computer making an error of that nature is astronomical, but there is a nagging doubt. The phenomenon of distrusting computer output is described by Sanders.[19]

A second cultural bias has to do with the nature of operating a computer. Up until a few years ago (and still in many places) one had to feed punched cards into a reader by hand in order to make the computer function. Most systems still require the operating of a typewriter-like keyboard. Many managers resist the idea of having a keyboard terminal in their office because they feel it makes them look like a secretary. One must remember that our culture is one that regards gardening for a living as a lower class activity, but gardening for a hobby is sublime. Ergo, many managers believe that any work done with their hands is simply below them on the sociocultural ladder. Fortunately this problem may be solved by voice-activated terminals.

Perhaps the most difficult cultural bias to overcome is the prevailing attitude among managers that administration is an art. An art that is simply not conducive to automated data. The environment of management philosophy has been described by Easton as a broad river valley.[20] On one bank of the river are the managers who believe that management decisions should be made on the basis of experience, intelligence and gut instinct. On the other bank reside the managers who base judgments on decision-trees and computer-generated facts. In truth, of course, a good manager uses a combination of both experience and instinct, and performance probabilities that are suggested via automated means. The problem is basically one of ego in this case. Many managers feel that by using automated data for decisions they somehow devalue their own self-worth.

The Priesthood of Automation

When large-scale computers were just coming into the commercial marketplace, the story was told of a company (we'll call the XYZ Corporation) that had purchased one of these mainframes. The individual whom the company put in charge of this facility immediately had a multitiered glass partition installed around the machine, and established a super-clean climate-controlled environment. Within this partition workers wore head caps and booties. Of course later it was discovered that the computer did not require this kind of special care to operate properly. The operator had simply sought to increase the mystery surrounding the installation for the other members of the company. Thereby no one questioned procedures that were obviously beyond their comprehension. This was empire building in the finest tradition.

The situation in XYZ Corporation described above may not be as farfetched as it initially sounds. White pointed out that the historian Henry Adams observed at the turn of the century that the machine had replaced the church as an institution of worship in American culture. In his time the dynamo was the extent of technological innovation. In our time the archetype of technology is the computer.[21] If Adams is correct, the computer has all the essential elements that good religion contains. It jointly inspires fear, wonder and pride. Fear, because it is incomprehensible and unknowable to the uninitiated layman; wonder, because its operation approaches being magical; and pride, because although one cannot understand how the machine functions, he knows that it was the inspiration of others and fashioned with human hands. To extend the analogy, the initiated have a sacred language known only to themselves. One only has to listen to two computer scientists talking over a problem to recognize this fact. Last, the computer itself can be seen as an icon—a symbol of the elect. These initiated, these "elect," are whom I refer to as the "priesthood of automation."

Like the computer operator in the XYZ Corporation, there are many priests of automation who see this special knowledge as a way to gain power in the organization. Not only does this priesthood not educate management on the functioning of the automated system, but also make sure that management does not gain that knowledge. From this kind of activity, the priesthood can never be wrong, for their argument can always be that management simply is not intelligent enough to see the truth.

It is easy to argue that the nonuse of automated data rests solely on the head of uneducated managers. It is somewhat more frightening to believe that there could be those within the organization who would intentionally make the system difficult to understand. This is not to suggest that every automation specialist in every organization is doing this. However, it is possible that if a manager cannot get an automation specialist to give a straight answer in plain English, it might be that the person in charge of automation does not want the manager to know the answers.

Several writers have reflected on the problems of dealing with automation specialists in an organization. Donaldson, Stevens and Becket warn that the automation specialist "thinks of himself...as a computer expert, and will regard your business problems as tiresome distractions that come between him and his real vocation."[22] Montague has stated that libraries have brought this problem on themselves by not taking charge of technological innovation.[23] In other words, managers have allowed automation decisions to be made by the very people who have a three-piece vested interest in the outcome.

A compromise needs to occur. The automation specialist at today's technological level can build systems that produce data that are timely and understandable. The manager must be willing to pursue the kind of training that will ensure that the data that is produced can be utilized. As Orlicky suggests, the manager must become more of a priest of automation, and the automation specialist must become more familiar with the more profane day-to-day decisions that are made within the organization.[24]

The Rationale for Utilizing Information Derived from Automated Systems in the Management Process

The fact is that the computer industry has been rather good at demonstrating how various systems can make cataloging easier or typists type faster, but they have been rather negligent in showing managers how they can manage better. If one looks at many of the reasons why managers resist automated systems, he will usually encounter a motivational problem. Unfortunately either managers are motivated to use automated systems or they are not. It is unfortunate because the systems designers have given library managers little reason to be motivated. The purpose of the last section of this paper is to propose a reason for managers to use automated systems.

In an article, A.B. Cherns points out that automation can be used as a management tool for either centralization of services, or for decentralization of the organization. It can make centralization easier because it promotes communication of necessary administrative information from the line operations to the decision-makers in the organization. Thereby, the administrators can make decisions that are timely and well informed. Similarly, in a decentralized organization the problem tends to be that each independent section of the organization has difficulty knowing precisely what is expected of it. The improved communication capability of automation data can allow decentralized units to react to changing environments in a clear and uniform manner.[25] This paper will devote itself to centralized organizational aspects of library automation. It will be addressing particularly those who are library administrators, or those who wish to become administrators.

If one remembers the first section of this paper, the information flow from level-to-level within the organization was reviewed. It was found that one of the basic problems for the decision-maker in the organization was getting reliable information concerning the needs of the clients. There are those who would argue that this kind of problem is solved by instituting multi-level committees or quality circles where the line personnel can directly approach the manager with information. Unfortunately this still does not solve the basic deficiency, which is that the decision-maker still does not know the actual extent of the problem or the accuracy of the information. This is perhaps where the use of automation data has its best use.

There are two essential characteristics of successful management: superior information and superior control.

Superior Information

With superior information-gathering via automated systems, the organization can progress from being a purely reactive entity (i.e., only responding from crisis to crisis), to being an aggressive marketing organization. Thus, the organization can respond to situations before they reach the critical stage, or a phase that is damaging to the credibility of the organization. Information derived from automated systems does not just produce quantitative data, but has the potential for a direct qualitative effect on the library. This level of information produces better decisions, and makes the organization more responsive to client needs.

Superior Control

There is a second reason that library managers should consider making more use of data derived from automated systems. That rationale is that with information from automated systems, the library manager can gain more control and power over his organization. One somewhat hesitates broaching the topic because speaking of "power" with today's organizations being geared to humanistic models is considered heretical, or at least in bad taste. As a working definition I will define *power* as the ability to influence change in another person or group of people. In 1959 French and Raven did a good deal of basic reasearch into the types of power that can be exerted within a social organization. Their conclusion was that there are basically five types of power:

1. *Reward power.* The ability to reward an employee for correct action.
2. *Coercive power.* The ability to punish an employee for incorrect behavior.
3. *Legitimate power.* The employee believes the employer has a right to prescribe behavior.
4. *Referent power.* The ability of the employee to adjust behavior via identification with the employer.
5. *Expert power.* The employee adjusts behavior because the employer has some special knowledge.[26]

In 1981 Yuki further delineated these power bases within organizations.[27]

Up until about twenty years ago the library manager commanded power through the first three kinds of power described earlier. The manager was invested by the institution with legitimate power of position.

Some of the rights of that position included the almost total ability to reward or punish the employees for which the manager was responsible. The library, for better or worse, was in the hands of a single individual. That was twenty years ago.

Since then, a number of factors have affected this power base of the library manager. In probably one of the most cited pieces in library literature, Downs and McAnally portrayed the problems of the academic library manager.[28] On one hand the academic administration was limiting the resources and the privileges of the library manager, and on the other hand the library faculty were gaining more individual rights of employment. Although the library manager is still invested by the institution with the responsibility for effectively operating the organization, the institution has taken over an increasing array of budgetary decisions. One need not itemize the research on the loss of power of the library manager over library employees. The literature is packed with the joys of dealing with faculty status, collective bargaining and, of course, participative management. The library manager finds himself with the same responsibilities as twenty years ago, but without the ability to effect change either with the organization as a whole or with individual employees. In the modern library organization, rewards are given on the basis of union contract or committee judgment rather than by a decision by the library manager. Similarly, the coercive power of the library manager has been delegated to legal council and union steward. Many librarians are in one stage or another of seeing this phenomenon occur in their organization. The traditional basis for power over their organization is being eroded or is already gone.

What can the library manager do? The profession cannot throw out the unions or the committees because they are here to stay. This paper is also not suggesting that library managers give up trying to direct their organizations. What it is suggesting is that library managers must find a new basis for power to effect change. Since few of us are blessed with the charisma to lead on the power of our personality, that new power base or control must occur through superior information about the organization.

Salancik and Pfeffer have developed a model for gaining power within an organization known as the "Strategic Contingencies Model."[29] The foundation of this model is the fact that whoever controls the resources of the organization, controls the organization. Part of the necessary resources of an organization is information. This is where the library manager can exert new power. He/she can determine that his/her office is the only central collection point for management information and can determine who, when and under what circumstances that information will be distributed. Thus the basis for power for the future library manager lies in the area of expert power. The library manager will possess unique and vital organizational data available to no one else. As Pfeffer and Salancik point out: "It is the case that if one controls the information used in decision making, one can control the outcomes."[30]

The manager can further exert control over employees by using, or withholding, information. Meltzer has suggested that the psychological need-to-know is a powerful motivating force in organizations. By withholding information the manager can actually inflict punitive control over a given employee.[31]

The requirement for this kind of power rests in the ability to collect the information. This is where data gathering from automated systems is absolutely vital. Under present capabilities almost every aspect of a library operation can have an automated reporting function. As such, every library operation can have day-to-day—practically individual-by-individual—direct reporting to the library manager. There is no need for the constant filtering and refiltering of information presently available.

There are those who may think that this is too much like a chapter from *1984* or a sequence from *2001: A Space Odyssey*. But like many things, data gathered from automated systems is merely a tool. How library managers use this tool is largely a matter of personal discretion. However, the use of automation as a vehicle to effect change within the library is one of the last opportunities for library managers to exert any kind of control over the direction of their organization.

Conclusion

First, this paper examined the library as a marketing entity and discovered that most libraries are internally-oriented organizations. It was proposed that this orientation was due to the inability of libraries to adequately change with the differing needs of its clients. Second, the causes of nonuse of data from automated systems by library managers for decision-making were examined. It was postulated that this nonuse was primarily due to a motivational failure on the part of library managers. Last, the reasons why library managers should utilize data derived from automated systems, both as a way of directing the entire organization to a more client-oriented position, and as a means for the library manager to gain more personal control over the library, were examined.

In the final analysis, experience and instinct will ultimately mark the best library managers. However, good decisions are not only based on instinct, but also on the ability to formulate that instinct around quality information concerning the changing environment we live in. Rose has pointed out that the modern manager needs to be cybernetic as well as literate and numerate.[32] The responsibility of the library manager in today's society is more complex and difficult than ever before. While the demands on the services of the library are greater, the tools that the manager can use to meet those demands are fewer in number and more limited in scope. One of these tools is the kind of quality information that can be derived from automated systems. In order to carry out the responsibility, to do the job he or she is being paid to do, the library manager cannot afford not to use the tools available, including administrative information from automated systems.

REFERENCES

1. Runyon, Robert S. "Towards the Development of a Library Management Information System." *College & Research Libraries* 42(Nov. 1981):539-48.

2. Drake, Miriam A. "Managing Innovation in Academic Libraries." *College & Research Libraries* 40(Nov. 1979):504.

3. Miller, James G. "A Theoretical Review of Individual and Group Psychological Reactions to Stress." In *The Threat of Impending Disaster,* edited by George H. Grosser, et al., pp. 13-14. Cambridge, Mass.: MIT Press, 1964.

4. Meier, Richard L. "Information Input Overload: Features of Growth in Communications-Oriented Institutions." In *Mathematical Explorations in Behavioral Science,* edited by Fred Massarik and Philburn Ratoosh, pp. 233-73. Homewood, Ill.: Dorsey Press, 1965.

5. Horn, Roger. "The Idea of Academic Library Management." *College & Research Libraries* 36(Nov. 1975):464-72.

6. Andreasen, Alan R. "Nonprofits: Check Your Attention to Customers." *Harvard Business Review,* 60(May/June 1982):105-10.

7. Meltzer, Morton F. *Information: The Ultimate Management Resource.* New York: AMACOM, 1981, p. 6.

8. Shera, Jesse H. *The Foundations of Education for Librarianship.* New York: Becker & Hayes, 1972, pp. 394-95.

9. Divilbiss, J.L. "Problems of Teaching Library Automation." In *Problems and Failures in Library Automation* (Proceedings of the 1978 Clinic on Library Applications of Data Processing), edited by F. Wilfrid Lancaster, pp. 67-74. Urbana-Champaign: University of Illinois Graduate School of Library Science, 1979.

10. Toffler, Alvin. *Future Shock.* New York: Bantam, 1970, pp. 350-58.

11. Firnberg, David. *Computers, Management and Information.* London: George Allen and Unwin, Ltd., 1973, p. 20.

12. Posner, Michael I. "Components of Skilled Performance." *Science* 152(24 June 1966):1712-18; and Miller, George A. "The Magical Number Seven, Plus or Minus Two: Some Limits on Our Capacity for Processing Information." *Psychological Review* 63(March 1956):81-97.

13. Melnyk, Vera. "Man-Machine Interface: Frustration." *Journal of the ASIS* 23(Nov./Dec. 1972):392-401.

14. Lacey, Paul A. "Views of a Luddite." *College & Research Libraries* 43(March 1982):110-18.

15. Ennis, Philip H. "Technological Change and the Professions: Neither Luddite Nor Technocrat." *Library Quarterly* 32(July 1962):189-98.

16. "How to Conquer Fear of Computers." *Business Week,* no. 2731, 29 March 1982, pp. 176-78.

17. Rose, Michael. *Computers, Managers, and Society.* Harmondsworth, Eng.: Penguin, 1969, pp. 206-11.

18. De Greene, Kenyon B. "Technological Change and Manpower Resources: A Systems Perspective." *Human Factors* 17(Feb. 1975):52-70.

19. Sanders, Donald H. *Computers and Management.* New York: McGraw-Hill, 1970, p. 327.

20. Easton, Allan. *Complex Managerial Decisions Involving Multiple Objectives.* New York: John Wiley & Sons, 1973, pp. viii-x.

21. White, Lynn Townsend. *Machina Ex Deo: Essays in the Dynamism of Western Culture.* Cambridge, Mass.: MIT Press, 1968, pp. 57-73.

22. Donaldson, Hamish, et al. *Computer by the Tail: A User's Guide to Computer Management.* London: George Allen and Unwin, Ltd., 1976, pp. 45-46.

23. Montague, Eleanor. "Automation and the Library Administrator." *Journal of Library Automation* 11(Dec. 1978):317.

24. Orlicky, Joseph. *The Successful Computer System: Its Planning, Development, and Management in a Business Enterprise.* New York: McGraw-Hill, 1969, p. 4.

25. Cherns, A.B. "Speculations on the Social Effects of New Microelectronics Technology." *International Labour Review* 119(Nov./Dec. 1980):705-21.

26. French, John R., Jr., and Raven, Bertram. "The Bases of Social Power." In *Studies in Social Power,* edited by Dorwin Cartwright, pp. 155-65. Ann Arbor: University of Michigan, 1959.

27. Yuki, Gary A. *Leadership in Organizations.* Englewood Cliffs, N.J.: Prentice-Hall, 1981, 38-58.

28. McAnally, Arthur M., and Downs, Robert B. "The Changing Role of Directors of University Libraries." *College & Research Libraries* 34(March 1973):103-25.

29. Pfeffer, Jeffrey, and Salancik, Gerald R. *The External Control of Organizations.* New York: Harper & Row, 1978.

30. Ibid., p. 270.

31. Meltzer, *Information,* pp. 15-16.

32. Rose, *Computers, Managers, and Society,* p. 10.

MARY ELLEN JACOB
Director for Library Planning
OCLC

NEAL K. KASKE
Director
OCLC Office of Research

Management Information Systems in a Network Environment

What do the terms *management, information* and *system* imply? Management implies control, monitoring and some type of role. Information is more than data, and it is not always knowledge—it can lead to knowledge. The term *system* implies organization, order and plan.

In looking at a management information system (MIS), a system which supplies management information or information to management, we need to look first at the function of management. Peter Drucker has given a number of definitions on both management and the role of managers. One of these is: "Management exists only in contemplation of performance."[1] This suggests that management is not an end in itself but a means to an end, and that same aspect of it applies to management information systems.

Since we are librarians trained in engineering, the dual approach of a technologist and a humanist seems appropriate. Thus, combining system analysis with an assist from Rudyard Kipling's "Six honest serving men,"[2] we should examine the questions, what, why, when, how, where, and who. We at OCLC need to look at management information from several different perspectives, which we will discuss more fully under "who." But much of what we collect and provide must be from the library manager's perspective.

What

MIS's focus is primarily on allowing us to do a better job as managers—not to create a system for acquiring information. While this point has been made by others, it deserves emphasis, for too often its meaning is lost in the masses of data we can accumulate through systems, particularly through automated systems. In the OCLC network we process approximately 2 million messages per day, generating six to eight reels of tape or equivalent disc files.

Our problem with automated systems is not a lack of data, but how to sift through the mass of data available to find useful information, how to translate that information into knowledge that will enable us to make better decisions, and how to better plan, monitor and control the use, growth and development of the systems.

We need to segregate those things that we should examine in detail from those things we can look at in aggregate. There is really little point in reviewing transactions that fall within the norms. On the other hand, for those transactions that lie outside the norms, we may need to look at detailed information to ascertain the reasons for their abnormality. For example, if it appears that all books on an order which take longer than nine weeks to receive are books coming from overseas, we may want to add some different parameters that allow extra time for such books. Maybe the only books we want to select are ones that take longer than twelve weeks (i.e., we may need different norms for different classes of materials). The same idea can apply to cataloging of materials. Different formats and/or different subject areas may require different amounts of time and effort.

We can ask many questions of management information systems, and we can get many answers, but are we asking the right questions? What do we need to know to improve the operation of our libraries, and for whom— the library manager, library staff or user?

Too often the tendency has been to focus on suboptimization (e.g., to make acquisitions or the cataloging process happen in the fastest possible manner). More recently, technical services departments have sought to ensure that materials move through the technical services area *in toto* in the fastest possible way, rather than moving them through quickly by individual subunits.

We really need to look at the overall library operation and not the individual parts. The process, from the request for materials (if our procurement is triggered on that basis) to the actual provision of the material to the end user, may be one parameter. We may be trying to provide materials in advance of requests. In that case we may want to see how successful our selection criteria has been. How many times has a particular item been used that we have recently acquired? If it has not been used at all, what are the reasons for its nonuse? Did we select correctly or not? How does this relate, not only to our current users, but to future users? These are all questions that must be answered, particularly in these times of limited budgets for materials and staff.

Why

Having discussed some aspects of what, we should also consider why we need information. What are our criteria for success? Do we measure them based on the number of books processed, patrons served or user satisfaction? We have few measures of satisfaction other than our use of statistics or surveys relating to users and nonusers. The latter information is difficult, costly and time-consuming to acquire. However, if the library were to become a community information source accessible to every home in that community, we could acquire considerably more data easier, and in a more timely manner. Mr. Dowlin has described one system with this potential—Maggie's Place—elsewhere in these proceedings.

For a number of years, and particularly in recent planning, public libraries have been focusing on user satisfaction as a major criterion. Considering the political process in which libraries are involved with taxpayer support, this may be an appropriate measure of usefulness for a public library.

Academic institutions have always felt that their facilities were established for current users as well as for future users; they were equally concerned about building a scholarly collection for both the present and the future. It is more difficult to anticipate and establish objective measures of how well the library meets that future use. We can only do it by looking at how well we have met the needs of scholars in building our retrospective collections, and can only hope to guess correctly about the future.

When

When we need information can often be as critical as what information, and why we need that information. Timing is, in many instances, determined by the nature of the process or by cycles within our parent institutions, such as a calendar or fiscal year. We have more control over information generated for our internal management needs. We often fall prey to the belief that we need instantaneous access to current information. Computer systems offer us two major advantages. They offer us virtually instantaneous access to much information, as well as access to vast amounts of data that can be readily analyzed in many ways.

Computers can offer us information in real-time, but we need to think carefully about that use. There are times when delays in our systems work to our advantage. In designing systems we need to consider how to provide that kind of tolerance. We may at times feel something is abnormal in relation to a present situation but, if examined later on a long-term basis, may have been a minor blip—no major problem. We need to build certain tolerance levels into our systems to provide this aspect, so we take action when needed, but not unnecessarily.

We also need to recognize that much of our data is historical—i.e., it is based on our current systems and technology and our present methods of use. When we use historical data to predict the future, we must recognize that they will predict the future only insofar as the future is like the past. But if conditions occur where significant changes may happen, we need to explicitly acknowledge such changes and estimate the impact they may have on our history-based projections.

This is one of the major challenges we face in designing online catalogs. Since much of our information is derived from catalog use studies, we must not extrapolate the limitations of card catalog access into a new tool (the online catalog). We need to separate those aspects of information-seeking which are not dependent on the tools used—but are inherent in the process—from those things which are really based on the form or medium used.

How

The focus of this clinic is primarily on management information in automated systems. Used carelessly, computer systems can increase our information overload so that we have too much information to make the decisions we need to make. Rather than reducing our risk, these systems increase our confusion and literally make decision-making impossible. On the other hand, if we use those systems to create normal patterns and ignore what falls within the norms (i.e., have the system select the items we should look at), we can reduce the volume of information and concentrate on matters that need our attention.

Computers have a fantastic ability to process large amounts of information rapidly and whittle the information down to important items of concern to us. To date, they do not have the ability, however, to make decisions based on that information. They can merely alert us to the fact that some kind of action should be considered.

In data collection we must focus on automatic means of collecting data which are a normal part of the process for a particular activity. It should not require separate actions or unique actions just to generate that data. If it does, we run two risks: (1) someone will forget to take the action to collect the data, or perhaps more likely (2) we will add to the cost of our overall processing by collecting such data. Information has a cost. We must ensure that the cost of collection and analysis does not outweigh the usefulness of the information.

Where

Management information is pervasive and affects all parts of our operation. We were asked to look at this topic within the context of the network environment. Consequently, we will limit our remarks mainly to this environment.

At OCLC much of our early work focused on acquiring only those pieces of data which we actually needed to run and support the operation— in particular, the information required for billing. The design of our systems from a management support perspective leaves much to be desired. We are trying to rectify that in the design and implementation of system enhancements, but more importantly in the design of new systems.

For example, a major function to be added within the OCLC Interlibrary Loan Subsystem version three is the statistics-generating capability that will allow users to document the kinds of activity that take place within the interlibrary loan operation for both borrowers and lenders. Clearly, this is only the tip of the iceberg. Much more information is available and could be collected, but it represents consensus among users of the Interlibrary Loan Subsystem for those items they consider to be important. One can identify similar needs within acquisitions, cataloging and serials control.

Another aspect of "where" relates to whether such analysis and collection are performed online or offline. Not all processing needs to be online. Where quick, short, unique answers are needed, online has advantages from both a management and systems perspective. If long reports are being generated, these are better done offline. Much depends on the manager's needs and time frame and the system's design and flexibility.

Often what is needed is not merely to see a library's performance in isolation, but to see that performance over a period of time, preferably in comparison with other libraries. The OCLC system has the capability for providing such comparisons.

Some time has been spent by OCLC staff in designing, in a broad way, a MIS. Whether the system will ever exist depends on the needs of our users, the priority they give management information as opposed to additional indexing enhancements, and new features for other subsystems including subject access. At the moment, management information seems to be a low priority. Thus, while it is highly desirable and could be useful to library managers, other things are more important.

We are doing a much better job of designing management information into the local library system from the beginning rather than as an afterthought. We have reviewed what libraries need to know in regard to local library functions, and how we can provide this information in a cost-effective manner. Libraries will be able to collect statistics on just about everything. The need, however, is to determine the key factors in terms of library performance, and to collect and analyze that data rather than collecting everything. This will only answer one of the questions I have posed, namely, how the library relates to itself, and will not give answers about how the library relates to other libraries. That information must originate outside the institution, and could be provided through the mechanism of the central system. Some work has been done in this area (e.g., the Council for the Advancement of Small Colleges has used the HEGIS data), and using input data from a library will provide information to the library on its own processing in relation to other libraries.[3]

Who

In looking at information from a network perspective, we need to consider the different types of people who require and use management information. Our preceding discussion provides the necessary background. We have the end user or the operator at a terminal. We have library management, regional network management or service representative. We have the network itself or the service provider. Within each of these groups are subgroups which need other types and levels of information.

The focus of management information systems has been, and continues to be, the manager. While that is important, our focus should be on how to achieve the kind of performance we consider desirable. If we were doing this, our focus would be on the individual operator and worker rather than on the manager. This change of emphasis is most important within automated systems.

Operators need instant feedback on what they are doing right and what they are doing wrong. Sometimes this feedback is merely the response—"The system did not understand your last command"—or it may be more complex, depending on the nature of the system. The operator should be able to ascertain performance measures for each session completed. Few systems presently provide these performance measures. This is the kind of information we should be designing into future systems.

Users of online systems want to know: How can I get the information I want most easily? What am I doing wrong? How can I fix those things that are wrong? Library staff are interested not only in those facts, but also: How long did I take? How much did I do? How well did I relate to what others have done?

Library managers may be interested in parameters associated with individual operators if they are immediate supervisors. Senior management is more interested in how the library is doing in relation to its past performance, trends and growth in activity, how the library performance relates to other libraries, and what are the means of focusing on those areas which deviate from the normal performance range so as to take whatever corrective action is necessary.

In addition, senior management is also interested in assessing "what if" situations. "If my budget were reduced 10 percent, how would that affect resources available for staff, serials, monographs, and other library activities?" Would it be better to take a 10 percent cut in staffing, in materials area or different percentages of cuts in each? Should one area be favored over another? Historical data and models can help the manager assess the impact these changes might have on the library and its operation. They are not a substitute for intelligent judgment, and one must always look at the underlying assumptions, particularly when using historical data.

Regional network managers are interested in matters very similar to those of the library manager—e.g., the past versus the present; trends versus growth; this network versus other networks; high and low usage, and the reasons behind such usage; errors and problems incurred by users with the system; and the "what if" situation.

Bibliographic cooperative management is similarly interested, but from a somewhat different perspective. They are interested in present activity versus past, in trends and growth, particularly in relation to system performance and future capacity planning. They are less interested in their performance versus other cooperatives, but are very interested in how different groups of libraries are performing in relation to each other and as a whole. They are interested in high and low usage, and reasons for such usage. They also have an interest in error prevention and operator problems. Again, models and "what ifs" can be used to pinpoint potential problems, their impact on capital equipment procurement decisions, and the timing of those decisions. While each level is not necessarily interested in the same information, they are still operating from a common base (i.e., system activity), and this relates back to how an individual operator uses and responds to the system.

If we give the terminal operator or user the kind of information needed for the activity being performed, it should be somewhat easier to pass along the information the manager needs, and so on up the chain of command. The important thing is to select for each level of use the items that matter at that particular level, and not to prepare a mere mass of data. It is to select information that helps in the decision-making process—as in the case of the operator—to improve his/her performance. In the case of the manager, to plan, monitor, control, and alter the operation of the overall system.

Research Activities

In moving from management information systems to the individual users, we will bring together two research and development activities taking place in libraries today. These research and development activities are those of online cataloging and library MIS. We will start by reviewing some of the initial findings, assumptions and research activities relating to both online catalogs and MIS.

Before discussing these areas, it is important to note the connection between management information systems and online catalogs or OPACs (Online Public Access Catalog systems). The connection between these two areas is that of cause and effect. Used together, they create an atmosphere for "user studies deluxe!" The record of use that is possible to create from an online catalog provides a library's management information system with accurate data on how the catalogs are being used by patrons. Catalogs are the key to library collections, and an understanding of their use would be a key to understanding library use. These online catalogs, however, have a number of barriers.

The initial findings discussed earlier come from a number of different studies. All of these studies have been conducted in part or in their entirety by the Office of Research at OCLC. These studies are on three major topics: subject access, terminal requirements (queueing), and the online catalog.

Subject Access Project

The subject access project's objective was to determine the features of an automated subject retrieval system that would support the present search tactics employed by library users. The final report for the project will be issued this fall as part of the OCLC's Office of Research "Research Report Series." This report, like the first one originating from this project, will be authored by research scientist, Karen Markey.[4] Two other papers on the subject have also been published during the course of this project.[5]

Terminal Requirements Project

The second study, "Terminal Requirements for Online Catalogs in Libraries," is being conducted with funds from the National Science Foundation. Its purpose is to develop and to test an algorithm for estimating the number of public computer terminals needed by a library to support an online public catalog. The results of this study will be published in the literature, and the guidelines for the use of the algorithm will be offered as part of OCLC's monograph series (Library, Information, and Computer Science Series). This work, coauthored by Neal K. Kaske and John Tolle, will be available in 1983.

Online Catalog Project

The last of the three study areas is devoted to the online catalog and consists of three major activities. The first one is reported by Kaske and Ferguson in a report issued by the Council on Library Resources, Inc. (CLR), the major funder of these three projects.[6] The second activity, "Online Public Access Systems: Data Collection Instruments for Patron and System Evaluation,"[7] which has just been completed, was composed of three basic phases. The first phase was to assist in the development of patron assessment tools. Phase two was to examine and compare several online patron access systems. The third phase recommended a uniform online catalog patron monitoring technique. Most of this report (phase two) has been published separately as the monograph *Online Public Access Catalogs: The User Interface*, by Charles R. Hildreth[8] and is available from OCLC.

The third activity is the Online Catalog Research Project funded by CLR and titled, "Online Public Access Systems: Data Collection and Analysis." The ultimate goal of this research is to improve, through the design and enhancement of online catalogs, the patron's ability to access information. The project is divided into three major phases. The first phase is data collection and analysis via patron questionnaires and focused-group interviews. The second phase analyzes the current patterns of use made of online catalogs via transaction logs and activity reports. The final phase evaluates and integrates the findings for library management decision-makers.

Initial Findings

An initial key finding from these research projects was that there are a number of barriers which prevent library patrons from effectively using (or in some cases from even using) online catalogs. The barriers are the computers themselves, the system's language, and the bibliographical information.

The first barrier is computerization itself. Many people believe computers to be complex and that formal training is necessary to use computer-based systems. Some fear that they may "break" the computer, or inadvertently cause the computer system to malfunction if they do not use it correctly. People also find the computer to be dehumanizing and, as a result, do not want to learn about it. Some say that computers put individuals out of work, and therefore, should not be used. Thus, the computer (or terminal) and how it operates is a basic barrier to its use.

Patrons remember using the card catalog as an old familiar friend. There are many people who prefer the card catalog because it is more private—i.e., others cannot easily see what one is searching. It is also easier to look scholarly while intently scanning a series of catalog card entries. In contrast, the online catalog is generally in a public area where others may easily view a search in progress. This may have significant implications for where terminals are located and how many are required.

Another barrier is that the operation of various terminals is somewhat different. One of the most frustrating things for individuals to overcome in first learning how to use a computer terminal is to remember to depress the return key so the computer will read the message that they have keyed in. There are other idiosyncratic characteristics about computer terminals, many of which become trivial when one learns how to operate them. But until a few basic operations have been learned, terminals may be as foreign to a user as a manual transmission is to one who has driven only an automatic transmission.

Another major barrier is the system's—or command—language. Here we must learn how to ask the computer a question and get an answer. Is it an $AU/$ and the first four letters of the author's last name, or is it something even more bizarre and complex such as A/T with the first four characters of the author's last name and the first four characters of the first significant word of the title?

Some systems have two levels of command languages: one for the novice—which none of us admit to being—and another for the expert—a level we have not yet achieved. How about that vast majority in the middle? To these the system acts as a barrier.

The third barrier is bibliographical information itself. It seems that no matter how often people are given lectures on bibliographical information, they arrive at universities and public libraries with either near full knowledge or no knowledge at all of how to interpret bibliographical information displayed on a 3 by 5 inch card, a COM (computer output microfilm) catalog, or information on a computer terminal. A lesson to learn here is that major elements of bibliographic records should be clearly labeled with words easily understood by the majority of users.

The barriers then are computers, systems language and bibliographical records. The first barrier will soon disappear as computer users become more numerous, be it via the home computer or classroom instruction. We should see real improvements in the second as we make system languages more understandable and "user friendly." The third barrier, bibliographical records, remains to be addressed.

Another initial finding is that while information needs are not all alike, there are two key elements. These elements are time available to research a topic and knowledge of the subject. Most informational needs have an attached time constraint. That time constraint may be only a matter of minutes or hours, or it may be open ended in the sense that it will last for years. An example of an informational need that must be satisfied in hours or possibly minutes is one expressed by the student who walks up to the reference desk and says: "I've go to give this speech next period on birth control. What do you have in the library on birth control? Or by a student who says: I have to have an essay ready by next period on the subject of the Falkland Islands. Have you ever heard of the Falkland Islands and, if so, where can I find information?

Other informational needs may develop over years. An expert on herbs and herb gardening, when traveling about the country on vacation or business, may take advantage of different libraries and examine their collections as to holdings. The individual will probably also make an effort to visit different herbariums. As the knowledge grows, the informational needs change indicating that informational needs are time related.

An individual's subject knowledge is important in satisfying any given informational need. The novice in a field needs a great deal of information—e.g., definitions and basic works. The expert, on the other hand, needs to find that last elusive informational package on a subject, held by who knows what library; and the information should be current— perhaps from the latest journals or other information resources.

Assumptions

With this knowledge that people's informational needs are time related, and that they are at different levels of knowledge on given subjects, we need to make some assumptions. We must start by reviewing previous catalog studies though they will be about card catalogs, book catalogs or COM catalogs—not about online catalogs. More important than the fact that the catalog medium is different is that previous catalog studies were only time slices; they were not longitudinal studies. Consequently, earlier studies have limited application to the design and use of online catalogs.

People do not perform "known item searches" for most of their informational needs. They do all types of searches in more than one library location (the college library, the public library, etc.) to satisfy their informational needs. Figure 1 shows that as the patron moves "across time" in different library locations, they will do many kinds of searches for information. For example, in the first library they may search under author, then under title, then under subject. They may also be knowledgeable enough to use titles as subjects, depending on the division of the catalog. If it is a dictionary catalog, this is done many times unwittingly. If a catalog is divided, a person looking for a subject item and only starting with the subject may use the title catalog or the author/title catalog as a subject catalog, hoping the first significant word in the title, minus the articles, will be the subject they are looking for. They then find a book with that kind of title, note the Library of Congress subject heading on the card and promptly switch to a subject catalog to find their subject material. If their information need is more than a few hours or a few days, people may move on to another library to search its holdings in a similar way. They may continue at a third and fourth library, again searching by author, title, subject, and by title as subject. To gain a clear picture of how people conduct subject searches, longitudinal time studies need to be performed.

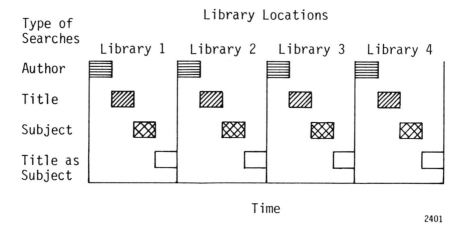

Fig. 1. Patron Searching Pattern Overtime

Transaction Analysis

Having examined some initial findings and having looked closely at our underlying assumptions, we should be able to provide some answers to our research questions—How are online catalogs being used? An overview of the related projects has been reported earlier. How do we obtain answers to these questions? Our solution is transaction analysis (TA).

The kind of TA we are going to discuss is not transactional analysis of the popular sense, but it is transaction analysis. The kind of TA we are discussing is the type that makes use of the transactions log produced by computers. This log is a record of the computer dialogue between the user and itself. These dialogues are recorded so that if computers fail, the transactions log can be used to recreate the processes, and by replaying them, bring the system back up from a "crash." This is done so people can continue to work as they were before the computers failed. The data elements that need to be captured so we can study them are listed and briefly explained in the following:

1. *Session identifier.* The unique identifier associated with the particular session being monitored.
2. *User identifier.* The unique identifier associated with the individual user being monitored.
3. *Database or file being used.* If relevant,the name of the file currently being accessed by the user in a given database.
4. *Date.*
5. *Time stamp.* The time at which each transaction occurs. Time stamps should provide as much accuracy as possible, although a time stamp resolution exceeding hundredths of a second is not generally useful. The point at which the time stamp will be applied must be specified. Ideally, the input time stamp should be applied when the user completes the input (e.g., depresses the Enter, Return or other special function key), and the output time stamp should be applied when the first character of output is delivered to the user. Since these exact times are not often available how the time stamps differ from the ideal time stamps should be stated.
6. *The source of each transaction.* Possible sources should include at least the terminal user, system and other transaction source (e.g., stored command files or operator messages).
7. *System-dependent state information.* If other information about the transaction is readily available, it should be included. Common examples include a transaction code generated to govern internal processing or special error or return codes.
8. *Blank space.* This is needed for state code assignment during post-session analysis.
9. *Length of text portion.* Number of characters in the input or response.
10. *Text portion.* Contains the text of the user input or the system response. The complete text is preferred when practical, but it may be truncated.

Why do we want to perform transaction analysis? The answers are simple: to have better online services, to provide better access to libraries, to make libraries respond to the informational needs of the public who uses them, to provide the dream—"a library at your fingertips"—and foremost, to make libraries the people's choice for information seeking.

Summary

In this discussion we have considered from our perspective how we define management information systems in the network environment and have considered Rudyard Kipling's "Six honest serving-men."[9] We have reviewed general concerns that apply to any management information system, but have also looked at this from the network perspective. We have focused heavily on users and their needs since they are the primary reason libraries exist. We have looked at the patron's use of online catalogs; have considered the barriers to catalog use, including computer knowledge, systems and command languages; and, in the organization, the content of bibliographic information. We considered informational needs as changing over time and with experience level. We have examined the impact of library location on the search type, and we've looked briefly at transactional analysis of the kinds of information that can be collected and some of the analyses possible.

Three other issues we will touch upon but not fully deal with are integration, privacy and power. We obtain management information not from one system, but from many external, as well as internal, sources. Presently we have left the integration of this information to the individuals. This lack of integration was a driving force behind OCLC's concern for designing a management information system that uses not only network and institutional information generated on the network system, but also allows the manager to draw on other information sources such as HEGIS, Bowker, census data, etc. In addition, it allows entry of other information. At present this is a dream, but it can become a reality provided librarians and managers believe such a system is useful and satisfies their needs. Without user support, it remains simply an interesting concept.

Privacy issues are many and varied, and have been discussed at some length in the library literature as well as in more general areas. There has been considerable concern over the problems of computers—i.e., their ability to amass and analyze information related to individuals. There have been a number of laws passed overseas and also within the United States relating to the individual's right of access to such information to ensure its correctness and validity. We must also consider these issues in designing MIS for any kind of monitoring of a user's interaction with a computer-based system. These issues are critical when we seek to monitor the activities and behavior of individual library staff members. How do we relate our management functions? And what right of protection or redress does the individual have in relation to such information? Management information systems represent power in this sense, and we need to ensure that proper consideration is given to the individual and his rights to privacy.

This, of course, leads us to the whole question of power within management information systems. As was indicated by Mr. Olsgaard, there is potential within management information systems for centralizing and controlling information, for restricting access to it, and, consequently, for it to be a source of power. While that is possible, it is also possible that we will see a democratization of information rather than a concentration and restriction of information as we are developing more computer-based systems, particularly microbased systems which are linked to a central database but which may act independently and maintain their own separate stores of information. That information will be more readily available to others who in turn can manipulate, access, analyze, reformat, and draw conclusions from such information.

Earl Joseph, a futurist from Sperry Rand, has stated that we have considerable difficulties with the development of distributive systems because we have no models. Our religions and our culture all tend toward hierarchical structures. We are not used to systems in which all parts are equal. The U.S. Government represents a departure from democracy in a political way. So too, distributed systems represent a new approach to systems design and to the potential for democratization of system access to and use.

We now face considerable challenges: how can we provide the integration of the systems we require and the information sources we need? How can we provide privacy for the individual with relation to his/her rights and privileges? How can we use power effectively—not to restrict information, but to make our systems work better and more effectively?

So, what do we see for the future? We will have the option of creating, internally, our own systems which operate on microcomputers or minicomputers. At OCLC we have used not only mainframe data collection and analysis, but also such microbased tools as Visicalc and Supercalc for both our system performance projections and preliminary budget analysis.

We will have access to information sources through such services as EDUNET and EDUCOM, including the HEGIS data. We will likely have library management-related services available from other information providers such as BRS and Lockheed, as well as OCLC and RLIN. Our challenge as managers will be to take those various information sources and integrate them so as to provide us with the information we need to manage our individual enterprises. The questions remain to be answered. How can we better manage our networks, our consortia, our libraries, to better serve our users both present and future?

REFERENCES

1. Drucker, Peter R. *Management: Tasks, Responsibilities, Practices.* New York: Harper & Row, 1973.

2. Kipling, Rudyard. "The Elephant Child." In *Just So Stories for Little Children.* Garden City, N.Y.: Doubleday, Doran, 1929, p. 85. "I keep six honest serving-men. They taught me all I knew: Their names are What and Why and When and How and Where and Who."

3. Council for the Advancement of Small Colleges. *Managing Costs and Services in College Libraries: A User's Manual.* Washington, D.C.: CASC, 1979.

4. Markey, Karen. "Analytical Review of Catalog Use Studies" (ERIC, ED 186 041). Columbus, Ohio: OCLC, Research Dept., Office of Planning and Research, 1980.

5. Kaske, Neal K., and Sanders, Nancy P. "On-Line Subject Access: The Human Side of the Problem." *RQ* 20(Fall 1980):52-58; and _____ . "Evaluating the Effectiveness of Subject Access: The View of the Library Patron." In *Communicating Information*, vol. 17 (Proceedings of the 43rd ASIS Annual Meeting, 5-10 Oct. 1980, Anaheim, Calif.), edited by Alan Benenfield and John E. Kazlauskas, pp. 323-25. White Plains, N.Y.: Knowledge Industry Publications, 1980.

6. Kaske, Neal K., and Ferguson, Douglas. "On-Line Public Access to Library Bibliography Data Bases: Developments, Issues and Priorities" (ERIC ED 195 275). Washington, D.C.: Council on Library Resources, 1980.

7. Kaske, Neal K., and Hildreth, Charles R. "Online Public Access Systems: Data Collection Instruments for Patron and System Evaluation." Dublin, Ohio: OCLC, Office of Research, 1982.

8. Hildreth, Charles R. *Online Public Access Catalogs: The User Interface.* Dublin, Ohio: OCLC, 1982.

9. Kipling, "Elephant Child."

BIBLIOGRAPHY

Altman, Ellen O., et al. *A Data Gathering and Institutional Manual for Performance Measures in Public Libraries.* Chicago: Celadon Press, 1976.
Association for Systems Management. *Management Information Systems.* Cleveland, Ohio: ASM, 1969.
Burns, Robert W., Jr. "Library Use as a Performance Measure: Its Background and Rationale." *Journal of Academic Librarianship* 4(March 1978):4-11.
Campbell, H.C. "Methods of Evaluation of Public Library Systems." *Public Library Quarterly* 2(June 1980):35-48.
Chacko, George K. *Management Information Systems.* New York: Petrocelli Books, 1979.
Curran, Charles C., ed. *Proceedings of the Library Research Round Table* (96th Annual Conference of the ALA, Held 17-23 July 1977, at Detroit, Mich.). Ann Arbor, Mich.: University Microfilms International, 1979.
DeProspo, Ernest R., et al. *Performance Measures for Public Libraries.* Chicago: Public Library Association, 1973.
Emerson, Katherin, ed. *Proceedings of the Symposium on Measurement of Reference.* Chicago: Library Administrative Division, ALA, 1974.
Golden, Gary A., et al. "Patron Approaches to Serials: A User Study." *College & Research Libraries* 43(Jan. 1982):22-30.
Hamburg, Morris, et al. *Library Planning and Decision-Making Systems.* Cambridge, Mass.: MIT Press, 1974.
Jacob, M.E.L. *A Simple Staffing Model for Predicting Manpower Requirements for Library Technical Service Activities.* Kinsington, New South Wales: University of New South Wales, 1977.
Kim, David U. "OCLC-MARC Tapes and Collection Management." *Information Technology and Libraries* 1(March 1982):22-27.
Koenig, Michael E. *Budgeting Techniques for Libraries and Information Centers.* New York: Special Libraries Association, 1980.
Kriebel, Charles H., et al., eds. *Management Information Systems: Progress and Perspectives.* Pittsburgh, Pa.: Carnegie-Mellon Institute, 1971.
Lancaster, F.W. *The Measurement and Evaluation of Library Services.* Washington, D.C.: Information Research Press, 1977.
Morse, Phillip M. *Library Effectiveness: A Systems Approach.* Cambridge, Mass.: MIT Press, 1968.
Peat, W. Leslie. "The Use of Research Libraries: A Comment about the Pittsburgh Study and Its Critics." *Journal of Academic Librarianship* 7(Sept. 1981):229-31.

Ross, Joel E., and Murdick, Robert G. *An Annotated Bibliography of Management Information Systems.* Cleveland, Ohio: Association for Systems Management, 1970.

Runyon, Robert S. "Towards the Development of a Library Management Information System." *College & Research Libraries* 42(Nov. 1981):539-48.

Wiederkehr, Robert R. *Alternatives for Future Library Catalogs: A Cost Model.* Rockville, Md.: King Research, 1980.

Wood, Judith B., et al. "Measurement of Service at a Public Library." *Public Library Quarterly* 2(Summer 1980):49-57.

ROBERT A. KENNEDY
Director
Libraries and Information Systems Center
Bell Laboratories

Computer-Derived Management Information in a Special Library

Introduction

Not the least of the benefits of automating libraries and information centers is the enhanced ability to monitor processes and services, to collect, structure, analyze, and report critical or useful data hitherto largely unavailable or excessively difficult and costly to obtain. Good management of information requires good management information—information that is as cogent, correct, current, clear, concise, and complete as cost effectiveness and enlightened decision-making demand. Computer-aided information systems offer not only opportunities to gain new insights into the services they support; they challenge the systems designer to build in the feedback necessary to control and improve the systems themselves.

The focus of this paper is computer-supplied management information in the special library environment. The particular context is that of an extensively computerized, corporate library network in a large research and development organization—Bell Laboratories.

Library Network Structure and Services

To help meet the information needs of its 24,000 people (of whom over 12,000 are scientists, engineers and managers),* Bell Laboratories has developed a multi-unit library system, structured and managed as a tightly integrated network. The present system is composed of twenty-five librar-

---

*All data, unless indicated otherwise, are as of April 1982.

ies, a half dozen special information services, and several supporting units serving nineteen Bell Laboratories and Western Electric sites in eight states.

The primary goal of the library system is to provide to all employees, however distant from company headquarters in Murray Hill, New Jersey, a full spectrum of information services of comparable high quality, at reasonable cost, quickly delivered. To this end, much emphasis is placed on networking, on functional interdependency, resource pooling, responsibility sharing, coordinated management, and commonality of systems, standards and goals. To help make networking work, a mix of centralized special services and decentralized standard services is employed, supported by substantial computer, communications, delivery, and management information systems.

Decentralization is preferred for the basic library functions, i.e., circulation and reference services, certain information alerting and online searching services, and the on-site supply of the book, journal and other information services required to handle promptly the majority of local information needs. Collection building, however, is not limited to local needs; each library has responsibilities to the system and, as will be noted later, coordinated resource management is one of the major targets and operational realities of the network.

Centralized services encompass functions and resources needed throughout the network that would be inefficient or uneconomical or impossible to provide on a local level. Centralization also offers opportunities for introducing and insuring common high standards and system-wide service monitoring, as well as supplying the critical mass and economies of scale necessary to justify certain specialized endeavors. Among the operations that are centralized, but not all at one location, are:

—acquisition, classification, cataloging, and the building and maintenance of network databases for books, journals, internal technical documents, and other resources;

—information alerting services, including the regular publication of thirteen major announcement bulletins, a computer-aided system for selectively disseminating internal technical documents, and an emerging electronic bulletin system;

—publication of a diversity of specialized information directories, catalogs, indexes, pathfinders, and so forth;

—information retrieval services using highly trained subject specialists, skilled in machine and manual searching, to undertake the more demanding information searches of both bibliographic and numeric databases, compile specific and continuing bibliographies, and supplement reference librarian services;

—computing information services, including specialized announcement and index services, the handling of external requests for Bell Labs software, and the operation of libraries specializing in computer information to support numerous computing activities;

—technical report services furnishing centrally a full range of acquisition, announcement, request processing, and search services on domestic and foreign technical reports of interest to Bell Labs;

—translation services providing oral and written translations by on-site staff or external assignment of all the major languages of science;

—management information services, as outlined in part below, supplying an extensive series of computer-compiled reports on library operations and performance;

—copyright royalty payment operations; and

—information system design and development services charged with the primary responsibility for designing, programming and establishing new and improved information handling systems for the whole network.

Computer Systems

Supporting these services and almost every facet of library operations is a complex of computer systems developed by the Bell Labs libraries since the mid-1960s. The principal computer-aided functions and systems are listed in figures 1 and 2 respectively. We shall note only sufficient details about these systems to help place in proper perspective the *information management information* they have been designed to provide. Additional details about some of the systems and services are contained in an earlier paper and its references.[1]

Management Information

We shall address, in turn, examples of management information relating to book selection, acquisitions, financial accounting, and cataloging; serials control; information alerting, copying and royalty payments; circulation operations, supply services, and resource management; and finally, some retrieval services.

First, we shall discuss book selection. Two major imperatives apply to collection building in a library network that operates as an integrated system rather than as a loose consortium of essentially separate enterprises: meeting local needs *and* coordinating total resources in a service- and cost-effective way. Both these requirements have been significantly aided by a computer-supported selection system implemented in Bell Laboratories in 1975. In this system, used for both selection and weeding purposes, "selection profiles" have been established for each library. These define

COLLECTION BUILDING AND UPKEEP

CATALOGING AND INDEXING

INFORMATION ALERTING

DOCUMENT DISSEMINATION

CIRCULATION CONTROL AND REQUEST PROCESSING

INFORMATION RETRIEVAL

PREPARATION OF PUBLICATIONS

TEXT COMPOSITION AND EDITING

SERVICE MONITORING AND MANAGEMENT FEEDBACK

FISCAL CONTROL

NETWORKING

COPYRIGHT ROYALTY PAYMENT

Fig. 1. Computer-Aided Functions in Bell Labs Library Network

not only the precise subject interest of the location served but the degree of coverage or "collection level" appropriate for that library. Much pertinent management information, including extensive statistical data available from the network's online circulation system on subject usage by technical departments and locations, together with input obtained from users directly and other sources, contribute to the determination of interests. Interests are defined by descriptor and classification number. Collection levels are expressed numerically: $0 =$ not yet defined; $1 =$ a representative, basic collection; $2 =$ research-level coverage; and 3 implies all worthwhile information published worldwide to support long-term research and development interests. For every library, a profile statement and subject index are computer-produced. Figure 3 is a portion of one library's statement showing, for example, a level 3 interest in solid state physics. To help coordinate selection on a total network basis, the overall subject interests of all libraries are maintained in a master matrix, available to all, showing the profile level for each library in each subject class. In figure 4, the example, solid state physics (530.4), is shown to be an interest shared on various levels by nine libraries.

BELLTIP   Book Acquisition and Cataloging System

BELLSER   Serial Acquisition and Processing System

BELLREL   Loan and Query System

BELLCAT   Catalog Search System

BELLPAR   Publication Announcement System

BELLTAB   Technical Report Announcement System

MERCURY   Internal Document Dissemination System

BELLPULL   Internal Document Request Processing System

BELLPAY   Copyright Royalty Accounting System

BELLCALL   Online Shelflist

BELDEX   Indexing System

Fig. 2. Computer-Aided Information Systems in Bell Labs Library Network

Management information systems should, of course, provide periodic checks or analyses to reveal if they are being properly used. The selection profile system has several reports of this kind. One is a "Dollars by Dewey" performance report (see fig. 5) which shows for each subject, the number of items purchased and the dollars spent by each library/level. Total titles held by each library are also given. A companion analysis identifies all purchases made at the zero (undefined) level—a situation compelling attention at profile review time.

Items selected for network libraries under the coordinated profile system are submitted to the BELLTIP book acquisition, accounting and cataloging system operational since January 1972. In this system, input terminals coupled to a large central computer submit order information, receipt and invoice data, cataloging details, file changes, and various queries. Output includes order forms, cancellation and claim notices, financial summaries, "in-process" reports, and much additional data that enable management to monitor purchases, work processes and other areas. Up-to-date process and accounting status reports may be obtained online from any of the many terminals throughout the network. Figure 6 illustrates use of the online in-process file facility to determine if a particular book has been ordered and, if so, its status. In this example, a keyword

MURRAY HILL LIBRARY – SELECTION PROFILE

SUBJECTS	DDC	LEVEL
Signal Theory (Telecommunication)	621.3804301	2
Simulation Methods	658.54	1
Size (Particles)	620.106	1
Social Sciences, Mathematical Models	300.18	1
Societies (Scientific)	506	1
Solar Batteries	621.475	2
Solid State Chemistry	541.042	2
Solid State Physics	530.41	3
Solid State Reactions	541.39	2
Solubility	541.34	1
Solutions (Electrolyte)	541.372	2
Solving (Problem)	153	2
Sound	534	2
Sound (Noise)	613.6	1
Speaking (Public)	808.5	1
Spectra, Infrared	535.842	2
Spectra (Organic Compounds)	547.346	1
Spectroscopy	535.846	2
Speech, Analysis	621.3819	2

Fig. 3. Selection Profile List

BTL LIBRARY NETWORK SELECTION – PROFILE LEVELS

LOCATIONS

DDC NO	AK	AL	CB	CH	CR	DR	HC	HO	HP	IH	IN	MH	MV	PR	PY	RD	WB	WH
530.1				1			1			1	1		2					
530.101					1		1											
530.12		1			1		2			1		2	1	1		1		
530.13							2					2						
530.143									1	1								
530.144												2						
530.2	1	1		1			1			1		1	1	1				1
530.3	1	1					1			1	1							
530.41	2			1	1		2			1	1	3	1	1		1		
530.5					1		1			1		2	1					1
530.7					1		1			1		2						
530.8												1						
530.85							1					1						
530.9										1		1						
531										1	1	1					2	
531.017									1								1	
531.3							1											
531.32							1			1			1	1				2

Fig. 4. Selection Profile Matrix

SELECTION PROFILE PERFORMANCE
(DOLLARS BY DEWEY)

DDC No.	Library – Level	Items	$	Titles
530.41	AL – 2	7	167.97	131
	HO – 2	9	200.72	127
	IH – 1	0	0.00	78
	IN – 1	1	26.26	10
	MH – 3	23	694.27	209
	MV – 1	1	40.05	49
	PR – 1	1	33.58	77
	RD – 1	2	44.22	82

530.41 Solid State Physics

Level 1 Representative Collection
Level 2 Research Collection
Level 3 Comprehensive Collection

Fig. 5. Selection Profile Performance Report

search was made for the book, *Soul of a New Machine;* two libraries are shown to have ordered and just received the item. Another online report is particularly useful in monitoring the overall status of items flowing through the acquisitions/invoicing/cataloging system of BELLTIP. This report, the In Process File Scoreboard, permits a manager not only to determine how many items are in any given status (e.g., on order, in cataloging, etc.) but to compare the current status with a selected earlier date, say one month ago, as shown in figure 7. Scoreboard reports not only book copies, or book titles as appropriate, but machine words—i.e., disk space in use—for the system manager.

Other insight into problem situations in the BELLTIP world—e.g., books remaining too long in a particular state such as cataloging or invoicing—is provided automatically in a series of specific offline reports. On the financial side, online accounting reports, not shown, give to-the-moment information on payments, commitments, budgets, and percent committed for any or all libraries specified. Supplier account information is similarly available online. Still another report, available in both online and offline versions, provides valuable information on vendor performance. This report summarizes average order costs, discount percentages, delivery times, and number of claims and cancellations for each vendor over a period of time; the document's usefulness to management in renewing purchase orders and maintaining effective supply sources is obvious and substantial.

Several of the information tools helpful to catalogers in managing their activities may be of interest. One is a simple online facility, BELLCALL, for determining if a newly-selected call number is already in use; the video display response identifies the two closest neighbors on either side (see fig. 8). Another tool, useful in managing the large, specialized subject headings authority database, is a periodic printout of all the headings used with a given class number (see fig. 9) and another printout of all the class numbers associated with a given heading. These instruments are helpful in developing standardized headings for the selection profile system, for reclassifying parts of the collection, and for adapting or refining subject headings to the specificity required in a high-technology environment. Still another management report useful to catalogers, but especially to library supervisors for collection management, is the Related Editions Report which identifies all the editions held of titles held in more than one edition in any library in the network; multiple editions may or may not be justified, but they should be scrutinized. This report, and another listing books by publication date, are of substantial help in keeping collection growth, and shelf space, under control. The principal management aids generated by the BELLTIP acquisitions, cataloging and accounting system are summarized in figure 10.

```
*online/ipf
09:01:51 Tue Mar 30, 1982

Welcome to the Online In Process File.
For help, type, 'HELP'.  To stop, type, 'STOP'.
You may proceed.

=k/soul machine

    1.    1   SOUL

    2.   55   MACHIN

    3.    1   k/soul machine

B-NO: 193390D  CALL NO: 001.64019/K46s          ISBN: 0-316-49170-5
TITLE: Soul of a new machine.
AUTH: Kidder, T.
PUBL: Little.
YEAR: 1981. 293p.    ED:               VOL:        LCCN: 81-6044

LIB.  REQU.  TYPE  O.D.  STAT  S.D.  A.D.  PO/VEN  INV  PRICE  B-NUMBER  SUB
DR01               2043   S    2063         07      P   12.55  193390D    01
CB01   TID    R    2063   S    2077         32      P   10.46  193390D    03
```

Fig. 6. Online In Process File Query

Please give cutoff date (today is 3728)
= 3698
The following copies are inadequate for order
326025A 1
326600A 1
The following titles are inadequate for cataloging
199297C

The In Process File includes:

	Total Now		Prior to Day 3698	
	# entries	# words	# entries	# words
Copies				
Requisitioned	136	3768	69	1608
On Order	3944	82550	2181	46012
Claimed	665	17864	476	13356
Standing Orders	51	1041	50	1021
In Cataloging	1193	34095	367	10255
In Preparations	1179	35634	35	1082
Sent	1842	55278	4	124
Sent Direct	104	3011	1	31
Cancelled	121	2823	0	0
Aborted	0	0	0	0
Titles				
Supporting Order	6208	345104	4547	260004
Orig. Cataloging	2524	166045	2083	140259
Catalog Changes	1271	27444	0	0
Invoice Traces				
	234	3723	0	0

Fig. 7. Online In Process File Scoreboard

Comparable to the BELLTIP system for books is the BELLSER system for serials acquisition, cataloging and financial control. One of its management facilities is called MONEY. This provides online displays of library accounts, vendor accounts and other serials data, including anticipated inflation factors for budgeting purposes (see fig. 11). The cost of serials in libraries supporting advanced technology explorations tend to be significant and demand close management attention to keep them reasonable. The cost problem is compounded in a large multi-library environment. One practice followed in the Bell Labs Library Network is to have a formal, face-to-face annual meeting of librarians to review serial orders and negotiate "adds and drops" in a coordinated manner. To aid this process, the decision-makers have much management information,

=001.6424P27/F79p

Nothing on file for call number #001.6424P27/F79p

Books with close call numbers follow

001.6424P27/E36p   +   0 153174

    EISENBACH, S./ PASCAL PROGRAM

001.6424P27/F49p   +   0 122510

    FINDLAY, W./ PASCAL

001.6424P27/G74i   +   0 176818

    GRAHAM, N. INTROD PASCAL

001.6424P27/G87p   +   0 149623

    GROGONO, P. PROGRAMMING IN PASCAL

Fig. 8. BELLCALL Online Call Number Facility

including circulation and alerting bulletin statistics, user reactions, etc. Especially helpful are two **BELLSER** reports: one an alpha listing of all current serial subscriptions and their prices; the other, a price-ordered list, high to low, of all serials (see fig. 12). Clearly, the high-cost journals at the top of the list get particular scrutiny.

Strong emphasis is placed in the Bell Labs Library Network on information alerting and dissemination services. As already noted, thirteen different computer-compiled announcement bulletins addressed to partic- ular subjects and audiences are regularly produced. Supplementing these network media are a number of local library bulletins that focus on the special interests of a given laboratory location. Another major component of the current information alerting service is **MERCURY**, a computer- driven system for selectively disseminating internal reports. Electronic versions of the bulletins are also being developed.

How are these alerting services kept on target? Substantial manage- ment information is available to the editors, primarily from the computer

621.38413   621.384151   —   504 —

621.38413
- 3 Piezoelectric crystals
- 2 Piezoelectricity
- 1 Electronic equipment --Reliability
- 1 Filters, Electric- -Bibliography
- 1 Piezoelectric crystals- -Bibliography
- 1 Probability
- 1 Radio--Apparatus and supplies
- 1 Radio--Apparatus and supplies- -Directories
- 1 Radio transmission
- 1 Radio transmitters
- 1 Resonators, Quartz- -Bibliography
- 1 Statistics
- 1 Vibrators

621.384131
- 1 Radio transmission
- 1 Television transmission

621.384132
- 3 Vacuum tubes
- 1 Modulators
- 1 Thermionics
- 1 Vacuum tubes (High)

621.384133
- 1 Coils
- 1 Resistors, Fixed composition
- 1 Transformers

621.384135
- 3 Antennas, Dielectric
- 1 Antennas
- 1 Antennas--Data processing
- 1 Dielectric loss

504 —
- 10 Ultra high frequency transmission   621.384153
- 7 Radio, Short wave
- 6 Ultra high frequency technique   621.384156
- 3 High frequency transmission
- 3 Ultra high frequency systems
- 2 Data transmission
- 2 Digital communication systems
- 2 Radio reception
- 2 Radio telegraph
- 2 Radio wave propagation
- 2 Telecommunication
- 1 Amateur radio stations
- 1 Antennas
- 1 Frequency modulation
- 1 High frequency
- 1 Houses
- 1 Ionospheric radio wave propagation
- 1 Quantum electronics
- 1 Radio communication
- 1 Radio engineering
- 1 Radio waves
- 1 Solid state devices
- 1 Television broadcasting
- 1 Waveguides
- 19 Frequency modulation
- 2 Distortion
- 2 Frequency modulation

Fig. 9. Subject Headings Used with Class Numbers

- Selection Profile Management - Indexes, Matrices, Dollars

- Online In Process File - Order Status, etc.

- Online Accounting - Library, Budgets, Expenditures

- Online Process Overview (Scoreboard)

- Monitoring/Action Reports - Ordering, Cataloging, Invoicing, etc.

- Vendor Performance Analysis

- Call Number Usage (BELLCALL)

- Subject Heading/Classification Number Analyses

- Related Editions, Dated Publications

Fig. 10. Some Management Aids from the BELLTIP Acquisitions, Cataloging, Accounting System

- Displays library accounts for serials

  — Expenditures, encumbrances, budgets, % committed

  — For all libraries, some, or single library

- Displays vendor accounts

  — For all or specified vendors

  — For all or specified libraries

- Displays vendor inflation factor

  — For all or specified vendors

- Handles online changes in cost and budget data

Fig. 11. MONEY, an Online Management Information Facility in the BELLSER Serials System

```
244784v    Journal of Plasma Physics
           MH    1   MC    $    354.00
278640v    Theoretical Computer Science
           CIB   1   MC    $    350.00
           HL    1   MC    $    350.00
           IH    1   F     $    350.00
           IW    1   F     $    350.00
           PY    1   MC    $    350.00
210112h    Biochemical and Biophysical Research
           Communications
           MH    1   MC    $    345.00
237352n    Soviet Materials Science
           MH    1   MC    $    345.00
220770s    Dissertation Abstracts International.
           C. (European Abstracts).
           HO    1   MC    $    345.00
           MH    1   MC    $    345.00
278656m    Theoretical and Experimental Chemistry
           MH    1   MC    $    345.00
219584d    Cybernetics
           LS    1   MC    $    345.00
           MH    1   MC    $    345.00
215600y    Chemical Engineering Science
           MH    1   E     $    340.00
           PR    1   E     $    340.00
218896f    CRC Critical Reviews in Analytical
           Chemistry
           MH    1   F     $    332.00
200015h    CRC Critical Reviews in Biochemistry
           MH    1   F     $    332.00
279680a    Transactions of the American
           Mathematical Society
           HO    1   MC    $    330.00
           MH    1   MC    $    330.00
           WH    1   MC    $    330.00
```

Fig. 12. Price-Ordered Subscription List

systems used to process the article request traffic and to record copyright royalty payment obligations. The bulletin request program, for example, employs information about the journal and the requester (e.g., department, location) to compile a rich statistical record of usage; among the analyses routinely made are various rank orderings of the journals covered in the bulletins—by articles announced, total requests, announced/request ratios, etc. These data greatly assist in determining which of the many competing journals should be regularly indexed; although heavy use is made of external data sources, many journals must still be indexed in-house and careful attention to profitability is necessary. A similar approach is taken for the technical reports bulletin; analyses of the "hit" rates of each of the bulletin's many subject categories help in refining coverage and maintaining an overall hit rate of 80 percent or better.

BELLPAY, the copyright royalty payment system begun in 1978, provides further valuable insights into journal usage. One report from the system (see fig. 13) summarizes the demand for journal articles by time—i.e., by the date of publication. This provides a perspective of substantial consequence in managing costly serial resources.

We now consider the management information which the online circulation system (BELLREL) has been designed to supply. The principal reports are listed in figure 14. The most important is the Titles in Demand list, produced weekly to identify all book titles for which there is a total of five or more people waiting anywhere in the network (see. fig. 15). The two-line entry for each title shows the number of people waiting at each location, the number of copies available, copies on order (as learned from the BELLTIP acquisition system) or missing, and the ratio of copies to requesters in the waiting queue. (In figure 15, the book by Ball, *Algorithms for RPN Calculators,* has forty-six people waiting, six copies available or on order, and hence a ratio of eight.) Using this list, library supervisors hold a weekly teleconference to decide what additional purchases should be made to help meet demands and keep response time short. Counter balancing this "hot" list is a "cold" list, the Zero Activity Report, run at least annually to identify titles that have had little or no recorded use in a specified time span. This list, along with such other management data as the principal users of a given subject class, are distinctly helpful in purging the collection, conserving space and saving money.

Several of the other BELLREL management reports listed in figure 14 might be noted. The weekly Reserve Queue Aging Report identifies requests not satisfied within a specified time period because of some hangup such as the loss of the book. The Get Off the Shelf Report points to all cases where the system says (1) a request exists, (2) a copy is, in fact, available to meet the need, but (3) for some reason the item has not yet been

230320   IEEE TRANS COMPUT

	CURR	1 Yr.	3 Yr.	5 Yr.	10 Yr.	20 Yr.	>20 Yr.	TOTAL
AK	0	0	1	0	1	0	0	2
AL	45	10	3	1	4	4	0	67
CB	18	11	0	0	1	0	0	30
DR	38	9	1	1	1	0	0	50
EL	1	0	0	0	0	0	0	1
FJ	54	29	0	0	0	0	0	83
HL	3	3	0	0	0	0	0	6
HO	153	95	15	5	12	3	0	283
HP	20	17	7	8	8	1	0	61
IH	54	50	2	0	2	0	0	108
IN	15	34	0	0	0	0	0	49
IW	55	43	0	0	0	0	0	98
MH	166	98	14	10	26	4	0	318
MV	10	0	0	0	0	0	0	10
NP	8	4	0	0	0	0	0	12
PR	3	27	1	1	1	0	0	33
PY	27	26	0	4	3	0	0	60
RD	12	1	0	0	0	0	0	13
ST	2	0	0	0	0	0	0	2
WB	7	7	0	0	2	0	0	16
WH	48	19	1	6	9	2	0	85
XX	14	22	0	0	0	0	0	36
	753	505	45	36	70	14	0	1423

Fig. 13. Journal Usage Data from the BELLPAY Copyright
Royalty Payment System

supplied. Missing Item Reports, produced every two weeks in class number order, are used routinely to search shelves. In addition to these BELLREL reports, much other circulation information is available in a variety of correlations of subject, library, time, and borrower. One of these is the Loan History Report, a subject-classed listing of the materials borrowed by a specified technical department. This report is particularly helpful in establishing an appropriate onsite collection when a technical department moves to another laboratory location.

Information retrieval services at Bell Laboratories both supply and apply management information to good effect. Management information

- **Titles in Demand**

- **Zero Activity Report**

- **Reserve Queue Aging**

- **Get Off the Shelf**

- **Missing Items**

- **Circulation Data - Library, Subject, User Dept. Correlations**

Fig. 14. Some Management Aids from the BELLREL Circulation System

is, of course, often the subject of online searches. In addition to bibliographic retrieval, however, *bibliometric* studies are frequently a most
appropriate exercise of interactive searching powers. Quantitative analyses of a body of literature to assemble, say, data on the leading crystallo-
graphic journals or the principal contributors to the field of magnetic
bubbles, can be of much interest to information, and other managers.
Online searching also generates statistics helpful in monitoring and meas-
uring the systems and databases used, cost trends, searcher activity by
library and time and type of search, and so on. Extensive compilations of
these kinds of data are regularly given to management by the Bell Labs
Information Retrieval Service.

Conclusion

We have touched briefly on some of the numerous variants of management information reports that can be made available in a computer-
supported special library. Much of the satisfaction of working with
automated systems derives from power and responsiveness of the systems in
providing decision-aiding data. As most information managers recognize,
however, the very ease with which elegant compilations of all kinds can be

BELL LABS LIBRARY NETWORK TITLES IN DEMAND   07/21/78.   PAGE 12

RESERVES WAITING/COPIES HELD

DEWEY/ACCESS	AUTHOR—TITLE	AK	AL	CB	CR	DR	HO	IH	IN	MH	MV	PR	PY	RD	WB	WH	OL	RATIO	TOTAL LOANS
425/J83 109788X T IN WRITING.	JOSEPH, A. PUT I	4	5					6 3										2	43
428.3/B53D 136698K DOS, DON TS AND MAYBES OF	BERNSTEIN, T.M.	1	1										1 1-1			+1		3	51
428.7/A21 122512Q ING SKILLS	ADAMS, W.R. READ	1	1				1	49 +2										12	25
428.7/W14H:2 138769L HOW TO READ FOR SPEED AND	WAINWRIGHT, G.R.	10 1	1 1								1 1							4	22
500/D91E 145051P ENCYCLOPEDIA OF IGNORANCE	DUNCAN, R.F.H./	13 1			1		4 1	13 1		2				6 1		+1		5	20
501/H758 151088B TIFIC IMAGINATION	HOLTON, G.SCIEN		2				4 1			14 1			3	1		3		14	7
501/K965E 150129J TIAL TENSION	KUHN, T.S. ESSEN						1			4 1			1 +1	1 1	1			2	11
510.1/K97C 148555Y ENTARITY IN MATHEMATICS	KUYK, W. COMPLEM	1					2 1	3								+1		2	12
510.7823/B18A 151116L ITHMS FOR RPN CALCULATORS.	BALL, J.A. ALGOR	1		1			13 +1	5 1 -1		14 2+1			2 1	1	2	5 +1		8	6
510.7823/S61P 149023G GRAMMABLE CALCULATORS	SIPPL, C.J./PRO		+1	1 3		1	11 +2	3 +1		10 1+1			2 1	4 1	1	9 1		4	37
510.0/D81M 151091E H WORK OF CHARLES BABBAGE	DUBBEY, J.M. MAT						1 1			4 1								3	7
510.9/F55P 153985A PURE AND APPLIED MATHEMATIC	FITZGERALD A./						3			5			1					0	
510/L45I 154087L TROD TO COLLEGE MATH WITH A	LECUYER, E.J. IN		1				4 1		1	2			1	1		2		11	1

Fig. 15. Titles in Demand Report

produced may encourage excesses in reporting. The results may be unhappy (see. fig. 16).

Excesses in Information Supply, Frequency, Complexity

↓

Information Overload, Noise

↓

Information Disregard, Rejection

↓

Decisions On Assumptions, Past History, Hopes, Wind Direction

↓

Poor Management, Trouble

Fig. 16. Management Information Systems Perils

Professionals engaged in the uncertainties of the information transfer process, striving to couple information need to information source precisely, swiftly and economically, need all the help they can get. The value to information managers of a carefully defined, coherent management information program can hardly be overstated.

REFERENCE

1. Kennedy, Robert A. "Bell Laboratories Library Network." In *The Special Library Role in Networks,* edited by Robert W. Gibson, Jr., pp. 17-36. New York: Special Libraries Association, 1980.

JANE L. CALDWELL
Coordinator of Professional Activities
Bibliographic Retrieval Services

Management Information from Bibliographic Databases

This year's clinic dealing with the use of information for library management is very exciting. Perhaps the most exciting element is the fact that we are not talking in futuristic terms. The advent of the personal computer means that almost any library can afford an in-house database as well as access to outside databases. Sophisticated software, such as BRS/SEARCH, will soon be available for use on one's local mini- or microcomputer. This promises local access to the online catalog, an automated circulation control system, serials check-in, and the ability to store and manipulate library statistics and other types of management information. Libraries will have much better control of their own statistics and have surer methods to determine collection usage, user satisfaction, employee performance, etc.

Today, I am going to take a somewhat different, I hope, approach to the subject of management information than has been taken thus far, and describe information that is already available, easily manipulated and frequently overlooked. This information is available to all of those whose libraries are now accessing online databases through one or more of the vendors of online databases. Some of those vendors include BRS, Dialog, NLM, and SDC. There is a wealth of information available to the user of online databases that they may have overlooked.

First of all, what is a database? The simple definition is that it is a collection of data in machine-readable form. This data could be available in a batch mode or an online mode. I will limit my discussion today to online databases that are available on a dial-up basis from one of the search services I have mentioned. When I say that a database is available online I mean that it is possible to query the database, get results immediately and interact with that information all from a local terminal. An online database from one of the search services could have a hard-copy counterpart such as the ERIC database that corresponds to the print indexes of *Resources in Education* and the *Current Index to Journals in Education*. Sometimes there is no exact print counterpart as in the case of the Dow Jones database; sometimes, there is no print counterpart at all, as in the case of the Pre-Med databases. A database may be bibliographic, meaning that it includes citations, often with abstracts or summaries, to printed journals, monographs, technical reports, patents, etc. A database may be nonbibliographic, meaning that it contains data, usually numeric or directory-type information. A database may be full-text, meaning that the full journal article or newspaper story is available online. Examples would be the American Chemical Society's project to put their sixteen chemical journals online. Another would be the full text of the *Harvard Business Review* that will be available online from BRS. In libraries today, all types of databases are being searched to produce comprehensive bibliographies or to answer specific reference questions.

Online database searching began, at least in an experimental mode, in the early 1960s. In the late sixties some government-produced files, notably that of NASA, were the first to be made available in an "operational" mode. In the early seventies, commercial search services offered access through telecommunications systems to, at first, only a few databases. The number of databases has rapidly expanded and from one's terminal one now has access to hundreds of different databases. When online databases first became commercially available, the software was not nearly as flexible as it is now, response time as short as it is now, and the costs for an online search as low as they are today. When online searching first became popular, databases were used primarily to produce comprehensive bibliographies on specific topics. Later, as online search analysts became more proficient and searching became an accepted research tool, online databases were regularly accessed to answer the "quick" or "ready" reference questions.

Why use an online database to answer a reference question that perhaps could be answered from a directory or encyclopedia? The answer lies in the fact that with an online database, all the information from the record—some information that may never go into the printed version—is directly *searchable*. (There may be variations between the vendors of online services—it depends upon the way that the database has been structured by the vendor and what information has gone into the dictionary or inverted file, or basic index.) Information is available in an online database that is not available in a printed index (e.g., titles, journal citation, publisher's name, price, author's affiliation, funding agencies, etc.). Often this information could be accessible through a printed source, but it would be time prohibitive to find this information. Besides the obvious advantage of Boolean operators—*OR, AND, NOT*—or pull together synonyms or combine and remove unwanted concepts—positional or proximity operators allow the searcher to be more specific or to search for concepts that are too new to have standardized terminology.

So far, we are talking about what I consider to be the traditional approach to the use of online databases. Databases are primarily used to produce comprehensive bibliographies with the costs often passed back to the user. Databases are frequently used for reference purposes, often with the charges absorbed by the reference department. Usually money is allocated solely for this purpose and it is up to the reference department to determine if accessing an online database is the appropriate way to answer a specific question.

Not long after the introduction of online database searching, many librarians, and researchers in other fields as well, discovered that there were ways that online databases, and the statistics they generated, could be approached in less traditional ways to provide all types of information. Donald Hawkins wrote a paper in 1977, published in *JASIS*, describing some of these unconventional uses of databases. The title of his paper was "Unconventional Uses of On-line Information Retrieval Systems: On-line Bibliometric Studies."[1] In it, he described ways to use databases to quantitatively analyze the bibliometric features of the literature. By using online databases we can explore, at no great expense in terms of time or money, aspects of the literature in a specific discipline. Some of the characteristics of the literature that we can explore that will have great impact on one's life as a library decision-maker include information of an evaluative nature—particularly with applications for collection development. Other information is available such as information useful for planning future use of the library collection, information to plan and budget for use of library services, and information to use in predicting trends in book and journal publishing. Information from online databases can also be used to evaluate personnel—both library personnel and staff outside the department.

The obvious use of databases for library management is using databases with the subject emphasis on management, such as *Management Contents* or *ABI/INFORM*.

In my talk today, I want to take a very practical approach and describe ways that one can use online databases to provide information that has great implications for library management and for management of one's institution. I am not going to talk about the obvious—using databases with the subject emphasis on management, such as *ABI/INFORM* or *Management Contents,* that provide references to printed literature on management topics. Rather, I am going to discuss the use of databases to quantitatively explore aspects of the literature that have implications for collection development, for determining how clientele use the services, and how their use of the literature will impact one's library. I am also going to describe how the statistics generated by online database searching can be effectively used for planning, budgeting and evaluating one's library services. The information I am going to discuss today is available from other databases and other search services, but I will be speaking primarily of access to BRS databases. I am, of course, more familiar with BRS databases and slightly prejudiced toward BRS as an innovative search service. However, I do believe that BRS has been the most responsive to the needs of managers in developing extra services such as our collection devlopment service, faculty bibliography service, electronic newsletter service (BRS/Alert), and our online accounts file.

Getting back to the primary subject, I would like to show how online databases can be used for different evaluative or bibliometric studies. Online databases can be used for citation analysis which could have valuable applications in collection development.

Bibliometrics has existed as a field of study since 1917. Bibliometrics became more sophisticated when Bradford, in the 1930s, established a basic law of bibliometrics—Bradford's Law of Scattering. Bradford discovered that, by arranging journals in descending order of productivity of articles on some subject, it is possible to identify a "core" of journals that publish most of the articles on a particular subject. Trueswell took this one step further and suggested an 80/20 rule—20 percent of the journals in a given field account for 80 percent of the relevant literature. The manual work that can go into identifying some core list is beyond the resources of most library managers. Online systems can provide a method to simplify the identification of this core. Here is a method developed in part by Donald Hawkins, Jane Caldwell and Celia Ellingson:

1. Create a set of all journal articles on a topic. This would be a broad search to account for variations in terminology. Use paragraph qualification to make sure the articles themselves will deal with the subject matter rather than having the terms appear in the journal titles.
2. Sort by journal titles (if this feature is available on your search system—it is on BRS) and print journal citations.
3. Run the same search on all relevant databases.
4. Rank order journals by number of articles on topic.
5. Identify a core journal list/secondary journal list.
6. Compare lists with your own holdings to determine how well the core journals and secondary journals are represented.[2]

This approach will identify the core journals in a specific subject discipline. This is an abstract list in that it will not necessarily correspond to users' needs. BRS has taken this approach one step further and provides a

special service to assist managers in collecting relevant data for quantitative collection analysis. BRS will save all citations that are requested from
offline print requests for one calendar year. These offline prints are the
ones that have been generated in response to users' queries and should
represent the needs of actual users. Because users often use online services
when looking for information on new or "hot" topics, the collection
development service will represent current demands on the literature. BRS
will save the journal citations and generate an annual or semiannual
report, depending upon the service option that was chosen. The report,
broken down by database, will consist of two sections: (1) an alphabetical
listing by journal title; and (2) a rank order by frequency of citation.

   In my former life (before joining BRS) I was at the University of
Minnesota's Education/Psychology/Library Science (EPLS) library. One
of our continuing projects was the evaluation of our collection and we used
the BRS collection development service as one of the tools to judge the
strength of our journal collection and to identify specific titles that should
be considered for inclusion in the collection. This study was reported by
Celia Ellingson and Lori Hedstrom. Their methodology:

1. Select databases that are primarily related to the collection and are used
   enough to warrant further analysis. This limits the focus to ERIC,
   Exceptional Child Educational Resources, National Clearinghouse for
   Mental Health, and Psychological Abstracts.
2. Eliminate from study journal titles that were cited fewer than six times.
   This threshold was perhaps arbitrary, but it relates to the fact that
   interlibrary loan can be used for the first five requests.
3. Check each title with six or more citations for holdings information and
   location within the University of Minnesota libraries. Journals that
   were not located within the EPLS library, but had multiple campus
   locations, were noted for their location most physically available to
   to EPLS.
4. Count the total number of titles to determine the percentage held within
   the EPLS library, held in other campus locations, and not held.
   Example: Online serials list, like the California Union List of
   Periodicals (CULP), could provide an even simpler alternative.
   Example:

   ERIC

Total	544		
Held at EPLS	364	66.9%	
Held elsewhere	93	17.0%	} 83.9%
Not held	87	16.1%	

NIMH

Total	66		
Held at EPLS	34	51.5%	
Held elsewhere	25	37.8%	} 89.3%
Not held	7	10.7%	

5. Compile a merged list of all journals held outside the EPLS library, but within the University of Minnesota (twin cities campus) libraries. Example:

Architecture Library
  Planning for Higher Education (21)
  Progressive Architecture (14)
  Environment and Behavior (10)
Biomedical Library
  Journal of Autism & Childhood Schizophrenia (359)
  American Journal of Psychiatry (145)
  Journal of Medical Education (102)
  British Journal of Psychiatry (90)
  Behavior Therapy (80)
  American Academy of Child Psychiatry Journal (71)
  Journal of Nervous & Mental Disease (71)
  Hospital & Community Psychiatry (67)
  G/C/T (91)
  Bureau Memorandum (56)
  Pointer (56)
  AAESPH Review (50)
  Australian Journal of Mental Retardation (42)
  Psychologie a Patopsychologie Dietata (33)
  Child: Care, Health & Development (32)
  Teaching at a Distance (30)
  Special Education in Canada (29)
  United States Air Force RHL Technical Report (28)

6. Compile a merged list of all journals that were not held by any University of Minnesota library (checking holdings was a relatively simple process because of the existence of the *Minnesota Union List of Serials.* A student assistant was able to do the checking during his/her spare time).[3]

The University of Minnesota is one of the many libraries across the country that has taken advantage of the BRS collection development service. To date, most users have come from academic libraries, although there would be many advantages for corporate libraries.

Before I go on, I would like to review the assumption on which the collection development service is based and that is that citations retrieved in literature searches represent the actual demands of our clients. We have to assume that our users take the journal literature and the literature search seriously enough to want to read the articles that are retrieved. We have to assume that the users of the literature search service are representative of all our users. We also have to assume that the searches were relevant to the subject and that the literature represented was actually about the desired subject.

Surveys like the one from the University of Minnesota point out several uses for the BRS collection development service. It can be used to:

1. Judge the relative strengths of holdings within a specific library or group of libraries.
2. Identify core journal titles that should be acquired by a specific library.
3. Identify low-demand titles that could be cancelled if necessary.
4. Compare the requests of our users with other types of surveys that identify core literature in a specific field.[4]

The collection development service provides a quantitative measure of potential use of a library collection. It is not meant to be used without the professional judgment of the librarian or subject bibliographer. There are, of course, other factors to consider—i.e., the service measures only the requests from users of a literature search service. In libraries that charge for access to the service, these statistics would not represent needs of all users. In an academic library, undergraduate students would not be as well represented as graduate students and faculty. Rich departments that could afford more literature searches might be overrepresented. And, most importantly, the service is valid only in disciplines where online databases adequately cover the published journal literature and where journal publication is the accepted means of communication between scholars. The collection development service provides a quantitative measure of potential user demand and, when used in conjunction with qualitative measures, provides a rational method of collection evaluation.

Another online tool that can be used for a bibliometric study is the overlap study. Several years ago, I was involved in a study the goal of which was to compare overlapping retrieval between the ERIC and *Psychological Abstracts* databases. Before our study, we knew that there should be a high percentage of overlap between the two files in subject areas—such as educational psychology—which were equally represented in both databases. Our findings, published in the journal *Database*, June 1979, were surprising.[5] The percentage of citations that were duplicated...was less than might be expected based upon the percentage of overlap in journal coverage between the two databases...." After comparing the journal titles produced from the retrieved citations with the list of journals the database producers claimed to index, we discovered that "more than twice the number of citations actually duplicated could have appeared as duplicates." Our findings in the case of ERIC and *Psychological Abstracts* indicated that for these two databases, a search in a cross-disciplinary topic warranted a multiple file search.

At the time of our study, it was necessary to do a time-consuming comparison between the results of the several online searches. BRS now offers a unique feature—MERGE—that allows the searcher to merge together searches from multiple files. Duplicate citations can be easily revealed, and in addition to the obvious convenience offered to the consumer of the search, the MERGE feature offers valuable information on overlap between databases.

Often, it is a management decision to set policy on whether multiple files are routinely accessed to answer specific queries. The merge feature can assist managers, after studying results of various searches, to determine whether multi-file searches are necessary. In most library settings, it is often necessary to elect the most cost-effective single database search. Overlap studies and use of the BRS merge feature can be very useful to justify these decisions.

I have discussed uses of online databases to evaluate journal collections and the content of various indexes. There are several other nontraditional uses of online databases that can provide insights into the research habits of your clientele and thus better determine priorities of library service.

It is possible to use online databases to discover the research interests and citation habits of your clientele. Author searching can give you the subject specialities of your clientele, but by examining their citation habits through the use of a citation index like *Science Citation Index* or *Social Sciences Citation Index* you can unearth their ongoing research interests, the journals that they regularly scan (and probably subscribe to), and other authors that they favor. It is also possible to see if a researcher cites the same papers over and over again, or if he is adventurous and strays from his standard sources. It is then possible to speculate as to whether your library is really used!

Trends in publication can be determined by use of databases like *Books in Print*, Brodart's *Booksinfo* file and *Ulrichs*. It is possible to pull up all books recently published by a particular publisher to scan quickly their current output, or to take the opposite approach and do a subject search and determine which publishers favor particular subjects. Price information is searchable and within the capability of BRS files so it is also possible to use online databases to determine the average price of a book in a particular subject area, to determine what percentage of books cost more than a specific price, etc. It is possible to use online databases to determine how much literature exists in a topic before adding a new program or course in an academic institution. Online searching can provide the decision-maker with a starting point for justification of a book budget.

If the researcher cites papers from journals held by your library and not readily available elsewhere, or cites journals that you know he has requested or that have appeared in a computerized literature search, you can be relatively sure that the researcher has been using your library services.

To identify the research interests and publication output of an organization, search under the institution name to determine its publication output, see in what format it usually publishes, its subject area strengths, and related interests. Searching online is often the only way that institution names are accessible and it provides a quick and easy way to measure an organization's research activity. Do not forget to use files that cover patent information—often patents are the best measure of ongoing research in technical fields.

You can determine the "invisible college," or group of scholars who communicte directly with each other, by using cocitation analysis. Cocitation analysis is a sophisticated technique. For the purpose of discussion, we will simplify it to an examination of which authors cite each other. Because these cocitations are often based upon prepublication correspondence between experts, it is possible to speculate upon what core of researchers form an "invisible college." Computerized searching can make it possible to crack this core of expertise. Databases like *Science Citation Index* and *Social Sciences Citation Index* can be used to determine cocitation. Databases like *American Men and Women of Science* can be searched to discover experts in a specific field.

A different, and sometimes controversial, use of online databases is to use them to gather supporting evidence for faculty promotion and tenure decisions. Online databases provide a cost-effective method to quickly pull together complete bibliographies of all members of a department, whether in a university or other research organization. Individual productivity can be measured. The strengths of an entire department or organization can be evaluated and compared with similar departments or organizations. Databases that index material other than periodical literature, such as ERIC, NTIS, DOED, or SSIE can show evidence of the ability to successfully compete for research grants.

Citation indexes provide a way to determine the relative value placed upon the research produced by one's own faculty or researchers. Relative rankings or accreditation surveys of departments or of graduates of departments can be compiled by examining how frequently the department faculty or graduates are cited. Although it is possible to produce similar evaluation studies manually, online searching makes this type of survey economically feasible.

I have discussed how various types of "bibliometric" studies can be used to provide management information in libraries. Another aspect of online database searching is that it provides a sometimes overwhelming amount of information to library managers in the form of statistics generated by the online search service. The statistics, a byproduct of the service, provide information on who uses one's services and why they use them. The search statistics can provide cost figures—how much an average search costs in connect time, print charges, and personnel time—that can help the manager justify a budget. The annual increase in search volume can help one argue for an increase in staff—or at least justify the present staff. Sometimes it is necessary to use search statistics to determine which search analysts do not make cost-effective use of online time—perhaps it is necessary to invest in additional training.

I would like to review some of the information that should go into a search log, and ways one can use that information.

1. Search number. There are two different theories on how a search should be numbered. One theory is that a search should be a single intellectual query. It does not matter how many databases are accessed to answer the question. (The analogy would be that in traditional reference services you do not count each printed tool consulted as a separate search.) Another method is to count access to each database as a search. This is a better representation of the amount of work that is done, but it can be very misleading. Some institutions count access to different online segments of the same database as separate searches. A sensible compromise would be to keep counts of both.
2. Search requester. This could be keyed to keep track of department use and status of each individual user.
3. Purpose of search. Is this search to answer a ready reference question or to compile an extensive bibliography? Is the requester asking for information to write a short paper, to give a talk next week, or to review the literature prior to starting a dissertation?
4. Who will be charged for the search? Sometimes it is advantageous to be able to go back to your records to determine what departments have been using your services. You might need their support later! Another key point, if you are charging for your services, is to determine the level of support coming out of your users own pocketbooks.
5. Search question. A brief statement will do; it is helpful to code for broad subject categories.
6. Databases accessed.
7. Vendors used.

8. Prints—both online and offline.
9. Sign on and sign off time for each database.
10. Calendar day.
11. Elapsed time.
12. Estimated charges.
13. The name of a search analyst.

When the search comes back, one will want to add the actual charge and after the search analyst and requester have looked over the search, one may want to add evaluative comments.

Online search statistics, like statistics generated from traditional library services, provide hard data for library managers to use in evaluating their services and budgeting for the future. The difference between traditional reference services and online services lies in the fact, unfortunately sometimes, that a bill is generated each time we go online. For internal accounting procedures, we need to justify our invoice to actual services provided. This produces accurate record keeping because we are forced to log in parts of the reference process that are normally not recorded. Thus we can better judge the time it takes to handle a specific question and judge the costs of providing information.

BRS provides an online accounts file that helps searchers to tailor the search service to fit their specific needs and provides managers with the most up-to-date figures on online usage. The accounts file will display usage on specific files or access to all the BRS databases. The online usage will be broken down by current month, last month and the year up to last month. One will always have access to information that will help determine the online usage and expenses.

BRS, always trying to meet the needs of its users, is now developing an online record keeping system. It will provide a way for one to store this management information—the same information that would go into a search log. Monthly reports could be generated that will indicate how one is using online services, who is using the service and for what purpose, average time and cost per search, what databases are being searched, etc. Many libraries that have access to their own mini- or microcomputer already have the means to store and manipulate this type of information. The statistics online file will give all libraries that advantage.

I have discussed ways that online searching can provide one with a wealth of management information. Much of the information provided is *quantitative* in nature. This is not a negative feature for we need objective measures to evaluate our services. However, quantitative surveys should always be used in conjunction with concern for quality as well as quantity, and with the measured judgment of the trained librarian.

REFERENCES

1. Hawkins, Donald T. "Unconventional Uses of On-line Information Retrieval Systems: On-line Bibliometric Studies." *JASIS* 28(Jan. 1977):13.

2. Caldwell, Jane L., and Ellingson, Celia S. "Online Bibliometrics." *BRS Brief Paper Series* no. 4, June 1980, p. 1.

3. Ellingson, Celia S., and Hedstrom, Lori A. "Using Online Databases as a Tool for Collection Development." *BRS Brief Paper Series* no. 15, May 1981, p. 3.

4. Caldwell, Jane L., and Ellingson, Celia S. "A Comparison of Overlap: ERIC and *Psychological Abstracts*." *Database* 2(June 1979):66-67.

5. Ibid., p. 66.

BIBLIOGRAPHY

Broadus, Robert N. "The Applications of Citation Analyis to Library Collection Building." In *Advances in Librarianship*, vol. 7, edited by Melvin J. Voight, and Michael H. Harris, p. 299-335. New York: Academic Press, 1977.

Caldwell, Jane L., and Ellingson, Celia S. "Online Bibliometrics." *BRS Brief Paper Series*, no. 4, June 1980.

Garfield, Eugene. "Citation Analysis as a Tool in Journal Evaluation." *Science* 178(3 Nov. 1972):471-79.

Goffman, William, and Morris, Thomas G. "Bradford's Law and Library Acquisitions." *Nature* 226(6 June 1970):922-23.

Halperin, Michael. "Preparing Online Service Reports with Packaged Programs." *Online* 5(Oct. 1981):62-68.

Line, Maurice B., and Sandison, Alexander. "Practical Interpretation of Citation and Library Use Studies." *College & Research Libraries* 36(July 1975):393-96.

Narin, Francis, and Moll, Joy K. "Bibliometrics." In *Annual Review of Information Science and Technology*, vol. 12, edited by Martha Williams, pp. 35-58. White Plains, N.Y.: Knowledge Industry Publications, 1977.

EDWIN B. BROWNRIGG
Director
Division of Library Automation
University of California at Berkeley

An Online General Ledger System

Across academia, decision-makers with small to large budgets often have only the fuzziest idea of their actual budget balance, or what their balance might look like at some point in the future. Somehow, this situation persists with decision-makers who have an uneasy reliance on some kind of accounting process (sometimes automated), which generally they do not control directly. Typically, a manager's dependence on the so-called "accounting department" introduces an information lag of several weeks or even months. Thus, managers look at their budgets through a rear view mirror; and projecting their actual budgets into the future becomes an exercise in divination.

In January 1979, the University of California Division of Library Automation (DLA) found itself with the problem of maintaining a timely ledger. Also at that time, DLA was building a large-scale IBM operating system to support the University of California Online Union Catalog. This system also had all of the computing resources to support a sophisticated general ledger system.

So, an obvious issue emerged as to whether it was more cost-effective to buy, or to write from scratch, a general ledger program. Common sense suggested that it ought to be simple to buy such software. However, exhaustive investigation revealed that flexible general ledger systems came as part of a turnkey hardware/software solution. The fact was that the IBM/370 operating system proprietary software was either mostly batch, or otherwise required costly teleprocessing software which was not a part of DLA's intended software inventory. Timesharing was considered too, but even if the right software could have been identified and located, its cost would have been greater than writing the same programs in-house. The unexpected conclusion was that it was cost-justifiable to devote a programmer's time to develop an online general ledger system that would be tailor made to DLA's needs.

Nature of the Application

The essence of maintaining a general ledger is to create budget lines, to encumber and to expend against them, to have the balances of each line adjusted automatically, and to carry updated subtotals as well as a grand total. For example, if a general ledger were to have a line for "telecommunications," then its online implementation should support the following general functions:

—Associate the line entitled "telecommunications" with a fund code.
—Allocate an amount of money for "telecommunications."
—Adjust the allocation any time in the future.
—Encumber funds against "telecommunications."
—Adjust an encumbrance against "telecommunications" any time in the future.
—Allow full or partial expenditures against a particular encumbrance against "telecommunications."
—Allow expenditures from "telecommunications" for which an encumbrance was not made.
—Maintain a balance for "telecommunications," while adjusting the subtotal, of which "telecommunications" is a part, as well as the grand total.

Details of Implementation

The general ledger system developed at DLA has no name. DLA runs it under IBM's Time Sharing Option (TSO), and in theory it will run under any IBM/370 operating system. TSO handles communications with the terminal, but it could also be accommodated by CMS, CICS, etc. The application proper is written in PL/1. All of the programs were written at DLA by Michael Thwaites. File management is through sequential (QSAM) and basic direct (BDAM) access. For database management activities like indexing, much advantage is made of large regions of real memory. All transactions are check-pointed for restart. For simplicity and to keep costs down, dumb ASCII terminals are used in line-by-line mode. Through simple screen clearing, cursor addressing and a data rate of 1200 bits per second, a very friendly software interface eases the user through learning and use of the system.

Design Criteria

The design of the system takes into serious account the fact that the person who actually plugs numbers into it will want to do so without exhaustive training, but with ease, confidence and a minimum of time at the terminal. To those ends, careful attention was paid not only to the textbook functions of the general ledger, but also to the idiosyncrasies of the purchasing and accounting offices through which DLA operates, and to the preferences of those responsible for both the broad management and hands-on use of the system.

Detailed performance specifications were developed by a systems analysis team that included those mentioned earlier—the director and the programmer. The result was a printed document of some sixty-two pages that became the basis for the operator's manual.

Logging onto the system is a function that embodies many exemplary features of the system: brevity, ease of use, security, and selectivity. Within ten lines of text—99 percent of which is coming from the computer not the user—a session is provisionally established, most recent activity is recounted, the user enters the appropriate passwords, and limits of privilege are established based on the user's alleged identity.

In general, there are three levels of privilege: absolute authority to read and write anything (such as setting up fund codes, budget titles, grouping lines for subtotaling, and patching any number in the ledger). The next level of privilege is to encumber and expend. The least privileged users can only read the ledger.

The user communicates to the online general ledger in a command language. The number of functions is very finite and the command verbs are highly suggestive. To aid the user's memory, the system will issue an appropriate help message whenever asked to.

Because the system uses line-by-line terminals, editing is very simple. There are no function keys. The system allows the user to review a transaction in its entirety before executing it. Even if the user makes a mistake, it can be undone.

The online general ledger functions so as to reduce as much as possible problems with the mechanical aspects of the system. Not only does it do all of the arithmetic, but it also helps the user to verify that the right vendor is paid, and that only one payment is made to that vendor. It even allows credits and discounts to be posted to a particular purchase order to invoice. Output from the online general ledger can go to a terminal or be spooled to a printing device. When used in conjunction with an IBM 6670 or a Xerox 9700 online laser printer, the hardcopy output is particularly pleasing.

Limitations

One of the design criteria for the online general ledger was to limit its implementation exclusively for DLA. Nevertheless, other departments at the university can use it for internal ledger management. It cannot be used in a distributed fashion where several departmental ledgers might be aggregated, and that was a conscious design limitation.

Conclusion

The experience at DLA with a home-built general ledger system has been very positive. The director can look at the budget from his terminal any time he wants to, and see it up to the moment of the keying of the most recent purchase order and invoice information, which takes place virtually every day. It takes one person about twenty minutes each day to keep up with keyboarding. Since DLA has its own computer center, this system runs for no recurring cost of its own. But most importantly, it provides satisfaction with a bare minimum of human involvement.

GLYN T. EVANS
Assistant Vice-Chancellor for Library Services
State University of New York
Central Adminstration

ALBERT BEILBY
Acting Director of Education and Training
Training Department
Binghamton Psychiatric Center

A Library Management Information System in a Multi-Campus Environment

Introduction

The Office of Library Services in the Central Administration of the State University of New York (SUNY) has, since 1975, been developing a library management information system based on the analysis of library and other bibliographic and academic data which are available in machine readable form. Although primarily designed for the SUNY libraries, the processes are applicable in other academic libraries because of the general availability of the data used in the system. The task has changed over the years as new ideas and opportunities were realized, as new appreciations of the obtained results were attained, and as the technical environment has evolved. Nonetheless, the fundamental structure of the system design has not changed since the first ideas in 1974.

This is an interim report. Progress has been agonizingly slow for two reasons. First, the difficulty of obtaining support and resources has been a real hindrance; the work has been squeezed into overcrowded schedules and ever-straitening budgets. Second, many of the machine-readable data which one confidently felt would be available in the late 1970s or very early 1980s are still not available. Some years, at least, will pass before the work can be completed *as we see it now.* Who knows what new ideas and opportunities will emerge as new results become available? Nonetheless, enough has been achieved to justify this report.

Environment

The State University of New York is a multi-campus university in New York State. It is composed of thirty-two state operated campuses and thirty-two community colleges which are administered by local county authorities. The senior colleges in New York City and ten community colleges in the city compose City University of New York (CUNY), a separate organization.

The total student head count enrolled at the state operated campuses (i.e., excluding community colleges) in 1982 was 385,000, with 29,200 faculty and staff. The total collection size is slightly more than 10.7 million cataloged volumes, growing at the rate of some 400,000 volumes per year. The acquisitions budget in 1982 was slightly more than $12.8 million.

There are thirty-five separately administered and budgeted libraries within the SUNY state-operated campuses—the primary locus of these studies. They are composed of four university centers (including a law school library), four medical schools, twelve four-year colleges of arts and sciences, six two-year agricultural and technical colleges, four special colleges (forestry, maritime, optometry, and technology), and four statutory colleges (Alfred Ceramics, Cornell Agriculture and Human Ecology, Industrial Labor Relations and Veterinary Medicine libraries). All the variety one's heart could desire.

The Office of Library Services in the Central Administration of SUNY is charged with planning, developing and integrating the library resources of SUNY in support of its academic programs. In an early step to achieve this goal, the office contracted with OCLC in 1973 to provide services to State University and other New York participating libraries. As a result, the SUNY/OCLC Network is also administered by the Office of Library Services. The network now comprises 228 institutions (academic, public, school, law, medical, state agency, etc.) and for-profit institution libraries. A further 600 (approximately) are either sharing institutions or are members of processing centers or Regional Union Lists of Serials. Within the state, 70 percent of the independent higher educational institutions, 82 percent of public higher education, and 78 percent of the public library systems participate in the network.

As one of its services, the SUNY/OCLC Network stores and processes OCLC distribution tape records for its libraries at the SUNY Central Administration Computer Center. Currently over 10 million records are housed for the libraries, with the file growing by approximately 2 million each year. There is a clear relationship between this activity and the development of the library management information system.

It should be stressed that the Central Office of Library Services does not have responsibility for the direct operation of the campus libraries, which report ultimately to each campus president. The central office has a planning function in which it tries to create as hospitable an environment as possible for the campus libraries. The office is guided by Stafford Beer's dictum that "the only feasible ultimate objective of systemic control is to hold the system within its natural boundaries."[1]

Decision Support Systems

The computer has been seen as an aid to management from the time of its adoption by organizations as an administrative tool (as opposed to a research or production tool). It has been expected that data which emerged as a byproduct of (or could be coaxed from) a production operation would be collected, collated and analyzed to provide management with data which would improve the operation of the system. In library circles, circulation data seems to attract the most attention. It must be said, however, that recorded examples of such data actually being used to make decisions are extremely rare. A paper (such as that of F.H. Spaulding and R.O. Stanton from Bell Laboratories[2]) which records the effect circulation had on acquisition/selection decisions is a desert rose. Indeed, the development of management information systems seems to have created yet another battleground for internal control of any organization—well described by Peter Keen in his article "Information Systems and Organizational Change."[3]

The term and activity of management information systems is now becoming supplanted by decision support systems (DSS), the fundamental difference being that instead of providing passive displays of data (probably offline), a true decision support system goes one step further. The data are available online in a synthesized form from a variety of sources, and are presented to the administrator through a "friendly" terminal which supports modeling programs, color graphics and other facilities—all of which give the manager the opportunity to review the data and to test alternate strategies. King defines a decision support system as, "a computer-based system that the administrator uses to amplify or improve judgement. It is not a system that makes decisions."[4] DSS software has the following capabilities: (1) report preparation and inquiry; (2) modeling language; (3) graphic displays; and (4) financial and statistical routines. Hopkins and Massy write:

> The process of modelling is always one of synthesizing known facts, theories, and judgements into a meaningful pattern.
> Models are about something; they purport to represent an aspect of something that exists, or might exist, in the real world. We call the object of a model the *reference system*. Thus a given reference system can in principle be represented by many different models, each one more-or-less

accurate with respect to certain characteristics of the system....Models need to be verified...[and] validated....Models are designed for a purpose.[5]

They also caution readers in a manner similar to King: "A good model—one that is simple but complete, stable yet adaptable—should make the quantifiable dimension of decision-making a far less mysterious place in which to operate, but it will not thereby lessen the burden of choice."[6]

The task at SUNY has been to build such a model, although in truth the work began before the term and the attractions of the DSS were developed. Some results have been obtained from the work to date, although the project is not yet complete. DSS systems hold the promise of reducing development time.

Stimuli

The SUNY Office of Library Services did not begin this work on an idle whim. The libraries of the university were under severe fiscal pressure—and we had little idea then that the economic conditions would continue to deteriorate as they have. Since other institutions have faced some of the pressures, it is useful to list those seen as critical at SUNY:

1. *Acquisition formula budgeting.* The university had adopted the Clapp-Jordan formula[7] in 1968 and was using the formula to build the collection. In 1975, the formula was used by the Division of the Budget to cut back the acquisitions budgets for three of the university centers on the grounds that the libraries were, or soon would be "adequate" according to the formula. The loss of funds was two-thirds of $1 million from the annual acquisition base. Further, a derivative of that formula was being promulgated by the State Education Department as a state-wide guideline.[8] These actions were clearly not in the best interests of the university's libraries. The heat was on to develop another formula. As it happens, work had already begun on a discipline-based "formula," but was not complete in time to be offered as an alternative to the cuts in funds. (It is of interest that the results of a project by Evans, Beilby and Gifford completed in the process of developing an acquisitions formula, concluded that it is *not* possible to derive a "formula.")[9] It *is* possible to develop an information system which will reflect the bibliographic components of the academic mission of a campus.

2. *Lack of an adequate statistical database.* Apart from gross budgeting data, and biennial Library General Information Survey (LIBGIS) reports,[10] there was no firm database to describe the libraries, their collections, their successes, or their failures.

3. *Isolation of library data from academic administrative data.* Although library data were gathered from LIBGIS, and summarized from budget data, there was no link to relate them to academic program data such as the location and enrollment in courses and programs, level of programs (i.e., undergraduate or postgraduate) or location of programs. The chicken and egg question of the location of programs and location of library collections and which comes first could barely be asked, let alone answered. The one reliable element was dollars expended per full-time equivalent (FTE) student, achieved by dividing one number into another.

4. *Traditional library data emphasis on "inputs" rather than "outputs."* Apart from total circulation, and interlibrary loan (ILL) traffic, there was almost no emphasis on the collection of service data, which for a service organization is incomprehensible. (Reference statistics were added later.) LIBGIS surveys and the state guidelines emphasized space, facilities, staff, collection size, and collection growth, rather than performance. Not that those data are not important, they are. But one wants to know how successful, or useless, one's library is; its service, not its potential for service.) Furthermore, there was no evidence that the "official" requirements for statistical reports would change as machine-readable data became more available.

5. *The multi-campus environment.* Because of the multi-campus nature of the university, and because of the nature of the growing ties among libraries sharing the OCLC Network, it was clear from the beginning that any system design must accommodate that variety and that added dimension. Therefore, the system was designed from the ground up with multiple campuses and multiple academic programs and libraries in mind. Fortunately the program was prescient in that regard as fiscal crises have begun to force the "trades and affiliations" of academic programs within the university.

6. *Fiscal pressures.* The budgetary problems have already been cited. But there are other, subtle factors which should be drawn into account: the shift of monies to serials rather than monographs; new physical media; the growing necessity to purchase information-on-demand through database searches—or ILL—(as opposed to buying the potential to supply service through acquisitions); or the decision to retain or discard an item.

7. *Political pressures.* As would be expected, a sharp reduction in the acquisitions budget tended to attract attention to the problems with demands for a quick solution despite the absence of data.

A recitation of the earlier stimuli should not be interpreted as a criticism of the university or the profession. Rather it is criticism of the conventional wisdom, and the reluctance to accept both the need for data, and the need to absorb them into operational decisions. It takes an unconscionable amount of time and effort to effect change.

Given these stimuli, and the growing availability of machine-readable data, it was decided to build a library management information system which would satisfy the following purposes:

1. to establish a model that would describe the acquisition/retention process in a multi-campus academic environment;
2. to develop and refine the available databases for inclusion in the model—i.e., to rely on data which have been acquired as the byproduct of a production operation;
3. to establish computer programs which would drive the model and provide reports;
4. to provide individual campus reports and system-wide reports—including time-series and trend reports; and
5. to integrate the reports into the planning processes of the libraries and the institutions.

The uses to which the management information would be put include:

1. justification of acquisition budgets;
2. support of the planning process, particularly among:
   (a) academic programs and library programs,
   (b) campuses, and
   (c)campuses and their local disciplinary environments;
3. provision of specific campus/interdisciplinary reports by library disciplinary strengths and/or weaknesses;
4. support of the campus accreditation process; and
5. exploitation of the ability of the analytical programs to provide subject and/or form bibliographies by discipline for a campus, or group of campuses.

The Model

An early description of the model was reported in 1978,[11] but for the benefit of continuity it is briefly described here. The structure is that of the familiar five-box information system, comprising input, control, decision, output, and feedback (see fig. 1).

The central decisions in a library is the acquisition and retention decisions. The sum of these decisions is, in fact, the library. In an academic environment, the inputs into that decision are supply—i.e., what materials are available—and demand—i.e., what academic and research programs are supported by the library and for which community of users. The output

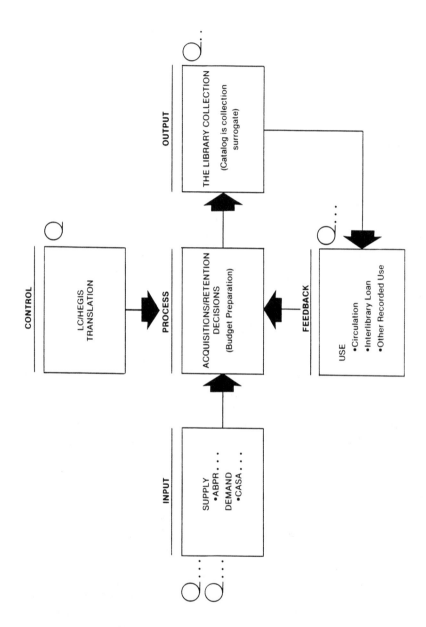

Fig. 1. Representation of the Five-Box Information System

of the decisions is the library, and the catalog is the surrogate of the library. The feedback into the decision (another source of input) is the use which is made of the collection, defined by the discipline and the community, and through the circulation, interlibrary loan and internal use. The control or program element is the software and tables which drive the management information system.

It was noted earlier that one of the criteria for the model design is that the machine-readable data to be used would be operational data. Such machine-readable data are available for each group described earlier although not at present in all SUNY libraries. The data are summarized as follows:

1. Input data (supply): Machine-readable files such as Bowker's Books-in-Print, or American Book Publishing Record (ABPR).
2. Input data (demand): Campus enrollment data described with the U.S. Office of Education, Higher Education General Information Survey (HEGIS) disciplinary codes.
3. Ouput data: OCLC distribution tapes containing local library versions and holdings of items cataloged into OCLC.
4. Feedback data: machine-readable files of circulation transactions from automated circulation systems; and machine-readable files of ILL transactions from online network ILL systems.

It is shown that with the exception of the Input Demand HEGIS Enrollment data, there is, or is likely to be, considerable consonance among the data files. They all are bibliographic data files, and will include, and transport, the same data elements among files depending upon the purpose of the transaction. All library files (Bowker, OCLC, circulation, and ILL) carry a Library of Congress (LC) classification number, and probably an LC card number and an ISBN. Three of the files carry, or can be made to carry, an OCLC number.

Files will also carry additional fixed field codes which assist in the selection of data for analyses, and transaction codes which define the nature of activity of the record itself. Examples of the latter are OCLC update, produce or cancel codes.

The data elements which are used for analyses (as opposed to the selection of records from a large file for analysis) in the segments of the programmed model are the OCLC number and LC class number, used singularly and in combination. Used by itself, the cooccurrence of the OCLC number is a measure of the degree of overlap among collections. The LC class number is an indicator of the subject strength of a library or a group of libraries. Using both elements in conjunction, it is possible to define both the collective subject strength of a group of libraries, and the degree of uniqueness or commonality of holdings of a library or all libraries within each academic discipline.

As data become available following the installation of automated circulation systems use, databased on LC class number and OCLC number will be derived from ILL and circulation transaction files and entered into the decision box as feedback data.

All of the discussed elements are well understood by library and information professionals, but the academic administrative data used as the "demand" segment of the input component of the model are less familiar. The U.S. Office of Education's National Center for Educational Statistics requires an annual HEGIS survey, through which all institutions report the number of degrees awarded, the numbers and levels of students and faculty, etc. To facilitate reporting, a disciplinary taxonomy was established in 1971.[12] SUNY has developed an automated statistical reporting system which uses this taxonomy, plus fiscal information in a Course and Section Analysis (CASA) file, to produce annual statistical abstracts on trends and costs within the university.[13] There is thus available a massive file of machine-readable data on the potential demand for library services by discipline and by the university community.

The immediate and obvious problem is that the HEGIS/CASA file does not carry any bibliographic data elements. However, the problem was overcome in the research project by Evans, Beilby and Gifford noted earlier which built conversion tables in which each term in the HEGIS taxonomy is expressed as a series of LC class numbers, creating, in effect, a series of mini-classifications. The ground rules are that (1) LC class numbers can be drawn from any part of the class schedules, and (2) LC class numbers may be used as many times as necessary. The HEGIS taxonomy has a two-tier structure in which major classes are divided into subclasses (see fig. 2). For its own statistical abstracts, SUNY has created a higher level amalgamation of classes designated as disciplines. There are ten such groups. The mechanism by which LC class terms can be assigned to a HEGIS subclass and subsequently amalgamated into higher levels is indicated in figure 3.

After the structure was defined, individual library subject specialists undertook to create the HEGIS/LC tables. It was found that over 13,000 LC classes were used to describe 494 HEGIS subclasses. (Figure 4 is a sample of entries taken from the African studies HEGIS class. The descriptions are taken from the LC class schedules.)

The use of LC class number, the HEGIS/LC tables, the OCLC record number and the campus code (OCLC's three-letter symbol) allows the identification of collection strengths and uniqueness related to teaching demands at any campus or within a group of campuses. Or conversely, their use can take a specific discipline or class and assess the relative campus strengths in that area. Since each record which is assigned to any

```
04    BIOLOGICAL SCIENCES

0400 Biological Science Unclassified
0401 Biology General
0402 Botany General
0403 Bacteriology
0404 Plant Pathology
0405 Plant Pharmacology
0406 Plant Physiology
0407 Zoology General
0408 Pathology, Human, Animal
0409 Pharmacology, Human, Animal
0410 Physiology, Human, Animal
0411 Microbiology
0412 Anatomy
0413 Histology
0414 Biochemistry
0415 Biophysics
0416 Molecular Biology
0417 Cell Biology, Cytology
     '
     '
     '
0499
```

Fig. 2. Example of the HEGIS Subclass Structure

class is individually identified, it is possible to create subject bibliographies by class to be used both as reference tools and for accreditation assessment purposes.

The Process

In a simplified form, the following steps are taken to complete the analysis:

1. receive OCLC tape;
2. read and extract the selected record use for analysis;
3. process the extract tape in the analysis program by (a) matching the call with HEGIS/LC tables; (b) assigning it to levels (i.e., subclass, class discipline, institution); (c) counting; (d) matching with CASA

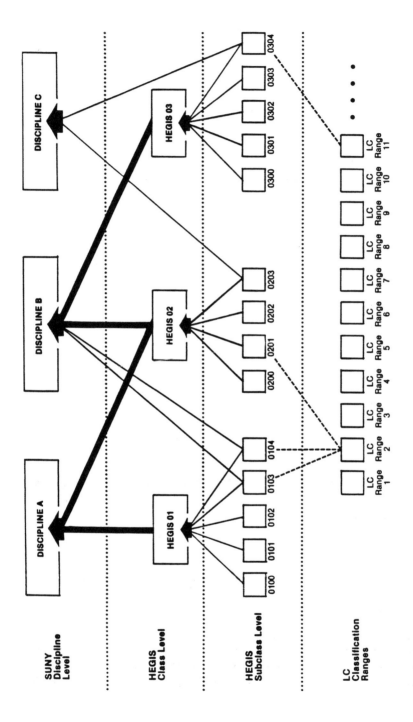

Fig. 3. Representation of the Mechanism by which LC Classifications
are Assigned to a HEGIS Subclass and Higher Levels

```
        ı
        ı
        ı
DT 730-995        History, South Africa
G 2425-2739       Africa, Atlases
G 8200-8903       Africa, Maps
GA 75-76          Africa, Mathematical Geography
GA 286-286        Africa, Cartography
GA 1341-1673      Africa, History of Map Production
GB 330-378        Africa, Physical Geography
GB 439-440        Africa, Geomorphology
        ı
        ı
        ı
GV 135-143        Africa, Recreation
GV 1705-1713      Africa, Dancing
HA 1951-2275      Africa, Statistics
HC 501-591        Africa, Economic History
HD 1169           Africa, Land Tenure
        ı
        ı
        ı
```

Fig. 4. Sample of Entries from the African Studies HEGIS Class

enrollment data—specifically student credit hours per HEGIS class; (e) performing overlap studies within each discipline at each level using OCLC numbers; and (f) reporting by institution and level, listing titles in brief entry of required listed titles.

Steps which are to be added to the process to complete the programming of the model consist of: (1) incorporation of publishing data; (2) incorporation of use data; (3) development or acquisition of decision support system software and evolution of system to an online interactive state.

The Results

Two analytic processes—components of the total model—are now operational at the SUNY Central Computing Center. They are component analysis and overlap analysis. Component analysis is a process in which catalog records from OCLC tapes are passed against the HEGIS/LC tables and allocated to subclasses, and the upward aggregates of class, discipline and institution. The analyses may also be correlated with the number of student credit hours taught in the discipline at the specific campus, based on CASA file data.

Overlap analysis occurs when the cooccurrence of the same OCLC number among the OCLC tapes of different campuses is used as a measure of uniqueness and commonality of holdings, and the grades between (e.g., held in three out of ten campuses). The overlap analyses are performed at the institution level, or, following a component analysis, at subclass, class or discipline level.

Results from these computer processes are designated as "obtained" results. The obtained results may themselves be subject to subsequent analysis, review and combination—as indeed they would be in a decision support system—to generate "derived" results. A start has been made on the process of producing derived results but by using the offline SPSS (Statistical Package for the Social Sciences) or manual analyses. Both obtained and derived results are reported in this paper. The derived results are sufficiently valuable to justify the target of achieving operational access to DSS software.

One major series of reports has been produced for the state university campuses, with data derived from those studies being the basis of all the results reported in this paper. In this series, the OCLC catalog tapes of eleven colleges of arts and sciences (four-year colleges), for the period April 1977 to December 1979, most with a small percentage of graduate (masters) programs were used. From this database, the study selected the latest use of monograph records which had a transaction code of *produce* and an imprint date of 1977 or 1978. This resulted in a base of 105,003 records for analysis. The attempt clearly was to gain an understanding of current acquisition decisions in the colleges. Other selections from the database could have as easily been made, ranging from the whole database to serials, updates and products. For our purpose, we chose the database we needed.

In the component analysis, the data were matched with student credit hour (SCH) data from the CASA file for 1978 (for which data are collected in the third week of the fall semester). We were exploring the academic demand at the campus for the 1978-79 academic year, matched with the acquisition of current (1977 or 1978) imprints which were received and cataloged by the library between April 1977 and December 1979. The data were analyzed first by the component analysis method, and then the overlap analysis method at all levels.

Component Analysis–Obtained Results
Figure 5 is representative of a typical page from a computer printout of the result of a component analysis. The four columns are respectively

the number of titles, the percent of titles allocated to each HEGIS/LC class for one campus from the database under review, the number of student credit hours and the percent of student credit hours for that campus.

The reader is cautioned that the first two, and the last two columns are added differently. The CASA/SCH data is a simple arithmetic sum. Either the students are enrolled in, say, a three-credit hour course, or not. However, because of the ground rule in the creation of the HEGIS/LC tables that it is possible for a class number to be assigned to more than one HEGIS class, it is perfectly possible and reasonable for a specific title to be allocated to more than one subclass in any one analysis. It is necessary for that multiple allocation to be removed at each step of the upward aggregation in order to avoid misleading and inflated results. Thus any multiple allocation of a specific record title will show as supporting the subclasses assigned, but will only contribute once to the class. A similar removal of duplication occurs at the upward aggregations from class to discipline, and discipline to institution.

This important point is illustrated in figure 5. The correct arithmetic sum for the number of titles in the class "Letters" is 4594, yet the reported number of titles is 4147. Given the consonance of the subclasses in the group, it is not surprising that such a multiple allocation can occur. Similarly, when the classes "Letters" and "Foreign Languages" are combined into a single discipline, the reported number is 5049, but the arithmetic sum (4147 + 1511) is 5658. This phenomenon also indicates an important practical consideration. If it is possible to identify for any one campus the subclasses and classes in which multiple allocation is taking place, the books which are bought are obviously lower-risk investment items than special areas of unique allocation—a nontrivial consideration in times of fiscal crisis. Finally, in column three the percent of titles is subject to the same rules of multiple allocation as the count of titles.

Component Analysis–Derived Results

One question raised by the component analysis is, simply: What is the percentage allocation between the SCH and the current acquisitions, and the ten-discipline HEGIS grouping? This allocation can be seen simply by charting the ten points for each discipline on a graph containing both acquisitions and the SCH. The results are demonstrated in figure 6. The result, which was startling, is that the graphs for ten of the eleven campuses were fundamentally the same as those shown by the three campuses in figure 6. The eleventh campus, SUNY at Purchase—the exception—is a new campus still busily building its basic collection. Thus the result is not surprising.

SUNY Grouping HEGIS Group/SubGroup	No. of Titles	% of Titles	No. of Student Credit Hours	% of Student Credit Hours	
Letters and Foreign Languages	5,049	21,500	19,346.00	17,800	SUNY Discipline Totals
11 Foreign Languages	1,511	6,430	3,130.00	2,800	HEGIS Class Totals
1101 Foreign Languages, Gen.	706	3.00	93	.08	
1102 French	172	.73	774	.69	
1103 German	94	.40	183	.16	
1104 Italian	116	.49	105	.09	
1105 Spanish	252	1.07	1,673	1.49	
1106 Russian	36	.15	36	.03	
1107 Chinese	10	.04	21	.01	
1108 Japanese	9	.03			
1109 Latin	4	.01			
1110 Greek, Classical	22	.09			
1111 Hebrew & Semitic	17	.07			
1112 Arabic	5	.02	78	.06	
1114 Scandinavian Languages	1				
1115 Slavic Lang. Except Russian	9	.03	3		
1116 African Languages	11	.04	9		
1191 Hungarian	1				
1193 Portuguese	44	.18			
1196 Persian	5	.02			
1197 Semitic Languages	17	.07			
1199 Foreign Languages, Other	13	.05			
15 Letters	4,147	17,660	16,339.00	14,610	HEGIS Class Totals
1500 Letters Unclassified			155	.13	
1501 English General	190	.80	57	.05	
1502 Literature, English	819	3.48	8,118	7.26	
1503 Comparative Literature	4	.01			
1504 Classics	81	.34			
1505 Linguistics	420	1.78			
1506 Speech, Debate, Forensic	19	.08			
1508 Teaching English as Forl	240	1.02	6,138	5.49	
1509 Philosophy	456	1.94	24	.02	
1510 Religious Studies	478	2.03	2,001	1.79	
1593 Technical Writing	10	.04			
1595 Children's Literature	219	.93			
1596 Literature of the Stage	654	2.78			
1597 American Literature	844	3.59			
1598 Mythology	174	.74			
1599 Letters, Other	5	.02			
1599 Letters, Other	1				

Fig. 5. Sample Computer Printout of a Component Analysis

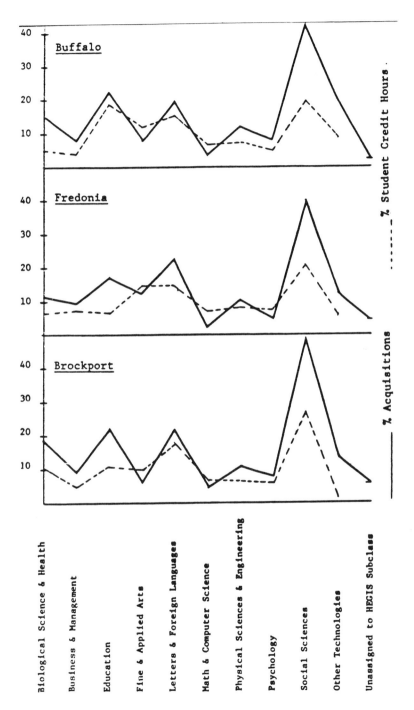

Fig. 6. SUNY Disciplines, Enrollment (Expressed as Percent of Student Credit Hours) and Percent of Total Acquisitions (having a 1977-78 Imprint Date) Assigned to the Discipline

In another test, scatter-grams were performed to examine the possible relationships between total credit hours and total titles acquired for each HEGIS class. In a scatter-gram, the coincidence of the values for each institution entered are displayed on the X and Y axis. The more the locations tend toward a straight line, the stronger are the relationships between the elements.

Table 1 shows areas for which very strong relationships existed between acquisitions and student credit hours. These eleven disciplines are now described as "immanent" program areas, proposing that there is an inherent relationship between the two elements. The third test undertaken with component analyses data was to examine the degree of multiple allocations among HEGIS classes, following the possibility of high v. low risk acquisition investment. The higher the index of multiple allocation of a title to more than one class, the higher the probability that the item will be used. An index of less than one would indicate a low correlation between the academic program and the acquisition program, diminishing as the index decreases. Table 2 shows the indexes for eleven SUNY campuses.

Overlap Studies–Obtained Results

The overlap studies (see table 3) examine the cooccurrence of titles among libraries based on the OCLC number at the subclass, class, discipline, and institution levels. The programs are designed for a maximum of ten institutions. This decision was frankly a programming compromise to obtain results quickly by avoiding the delay caused by the complexity of handling 100 institutions, as originally proposed. It has been found, however, that there is so little overlap beyond ten institutions that there may be little lost.

The results are displayed in a matrix in which the one column is the individual institutions identified by their OCLC codes with the total titles and copies in the last column. One column indicates the ten occurrences from unique (i.e., held by that institution uniquely), two (i.e., the institution plus one other), to ten (i.e., held by all institutions). The final column is the total of all titles. Each box in the matrix records the number and the percentage in each column. Table 3 reports the overlap for one campus and the total of all ten campuses among the subclass, class, discipline, and institution level. The holdings of one campus will not necessarily follow the pattern of the aggregate of all campuses.

The "total held by class" column is the sum of all copies held by a particular distribution—e.g., held in two or five libraries. The "actual titles" column is the number of titles which overlapped. This is best demonstrated in the ten-overlap column, where clearly the five titles held by ten libraries in the subclass will yield fifty copies (see table 3). Figure 7 describes graphically the overlap at the institution level found in this series of tests.

TABLE 1
Mid-Range Clusters and the Program Areas
for Which Strong Relationships Were Found
Between Acquisitions and Student Credit Hours

Program Area	r* p	SUNY Colleges		
SUNY—Biological Science & Health Professions	0.80 @ .004	Brockport Fredonia Oswego	Buffalo Geneseo Potsdam	Cortland New Paltz
Biological Science	0.97 @ .001	Buffalo Geneseo Plattsburgh	Cortland New Paltz Purchase	Fredonia Oswego
Health Professions	0.98 @ <.001	Brockport New Paltz	Fredonia Potsdam	Geneseo
SUNY—Fine & Applied Arts	0.86 @ .007	Brockport Geneseo Plattsburgh	Cortland New Paltz Purchase	Fredonia Oswego
Letters	0.76 @ .009	Buffalo Geneseo Plattsburgh	Cortland New Paltz Purchase	Fredonia Oswego
SUNY—Math & Computer Science	0.91 @ <.001	Buffalo New Paltz Plattsburgh	Cortland Oneonta Purchase	Fredonia Oswego
Mathematics	0.84 @ .009	Buffalo New Paltz Purchase	Cortland Oneonta	Fredonia Oswego
Physical Sciences	0.93 @ .001	Buffalo New Paltz	Cortland Oneonta	Fredonia Oswego
SUNY—Social Sciences	0.87 @ .003	Cortland Oneonta	Fredonia Oswego	New Paltz Purchase
Economics	0.88 @ .002	Buffalo Oneonta Purchase	Cortland Oswego	New Paltz Potsdam
Political Science	0.87 @ .006	Brockport New Paltz	Buffalo Oneonta	Cortland Plattsburgh

*r—Controlling for budget

It is one thing knowing the curve of the unique/commonality at the level described thus far; but it does not tell a library specifically how it relates to other libraries in the analysis. An extended report has been defined in which any one library can assess its overlap title-by-title with the

TABLE 2
INVESTMENT EFFICIENCY INDEXES FOR ELEVEN SUNY COLLEGES OF ARTS AND SCIENCES—1977-78 IMPRINT DATE

Institution	Index
Brockport	1.86
Fredonia	1.67
Buffalo	1.81
Cortland	1.83
Geneseo	1.63
Oswego	1.74
Plattsburgh	1.77
Oneonta	1.70
New Paltz	1.75
Potsdam	1.51
Purchase	1.64
Mean	1.72

TABLE 3
OVERLAP STUDIES

| Institution | HEGIS Subclass-Afro American Studies 2211 | | |
	Institution Code: XBM	Total Held by Class	Actual Titles
Unique	23	68	68
	17.42	9.48	33.66
2	21	72	36
	15.90	10.04	17.82
3	16	54	18
	12.12	7.53	8.91
4	10	48	12
	7.57	6.69	5.94
5	14	85	17
	10.60	11.85	8.41
6	11	72	12
	8.33	10.04	5.94
7	12	91	13
	9.09	12.69	6.43
8	11	96	12
	8.33	13.38	5.94
9	9	81	9
	6.81	11.29	4.45
10	5	50	5
	3.78	6.97	2.47
Total	132	717	202
	100.00	100.00	99.97

TABLE 3—*Continued*

Institution	Institution Code: XBM	HEGIS Class-Social Science 22 Total Held by Class	Actual Titles
Unique	3,214	9,091	9,091
	36.41	22.29	51.95
2	1,615	6,234	3,117
	18.29	15.28	17.81
3	1,106	5,178	1,726
	12.52	12.69	9.86
4	806	4,620	1,155
	9.13	11.33	6.60
5	671	4,065	813
	7.60	9.97	4.64
6	470	3,354	559
	5.32	8.22	3.19
7	376	3,087	441
	4.25	7.57	2.52
8	296	2,576	322
	3.35	6.31	1.84
9	181	1,647	183
	2.05	4.03	1.04
10	92	920	92
	1.04	2.25	.52
Total	8,827	40,772	17,499
	100.00	100.00	99.97

TABLE 3—Continued

Institution	SUNY/CASA Discipline–Social Sciences Institution Code: XBM	Total Held by Class	Actual Titles
Unique	4,228 37.88	11,262 22.97	11,262 52.52
2	2,176 19.49	7,850 16.01	3,925 18.30
3	1,356 12.15	6,222 12.69	2,074 9.67
4	965 8.64	5,452 11.12	1,363 6.35
5	798 7.15	4,825 9.84	965 4.50
6	545 4.88	3,912 7.97	652 3.04
7	439 3.93	3,598 7.33	514 2.39
8	336 3.01	2,920 5.95	365 1.70
9	213 1.90	1,953 3.98	217 1.01
10	103 .92	1,030 2.10	103 .48
Total	11,159 100.00	49,024 100.00	21,440 99.60

TABLE 3—*Continued*

Institution	Institution Code: XBM	Institution-Ten SUNY Colleges Total Held by Class	Actual Titles
Unique	8,241 37.80	25,474 24.26	25,474 53.88
2	4,167 19.11	17,256 16.43	8,628 18.25
3	2,642 12.11	13,281 12.64	4,427 9.36
4	1,938 8.88	11,776 11.21	2,944 6.22
5	1,521 6.97	10,035 9.55	2,007 4.24
6	1,166 5.34	8,700 8.28	1,450 3.06
7	884 4.05	7,224 6.87	1,032 2.18
8	666 3.05	5,776 5.50	722 1.52
9	405 1.85	3,771 3.59	419 .88
10	171 .78	1,710 1.62	171 .36
Total	21,801 100.00	105,003 100.00	47,274 99.95

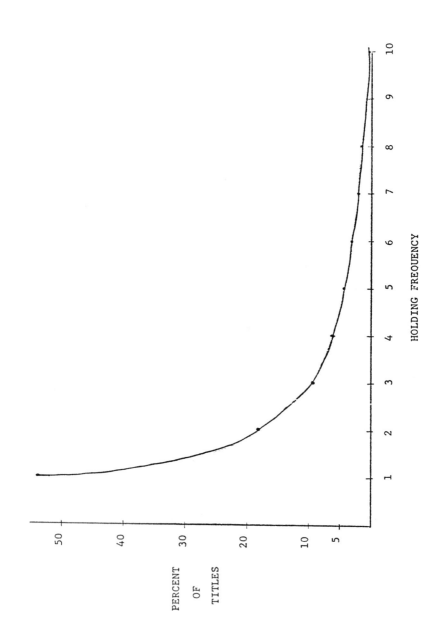

Fig. 7. Graph of Overlap of Titles at the Institution Level

other libraries. Figure 8 compares one SUNY library (Cortland) with the other nine in the analysis.

The last obtained report is a simple list of OCLC number of titles analyzed, with the OCLC holdings library code arranged alongside the number. This list is used as a crosscheck against the total results, but is also indicative of the ability of the system programs to produce bibliographies by library/libraries, by class, or by discipline. This facility has already been used to produce a bibliography of holdings in African and Afro-American studies for the chancellor's task force.

Overlap Studies–Derived Results

The overlap relationships can be described by five curves of highly unique, scarce, moderate, common, and ubiquitous distributions (see figs. 9 through 13). The distribution of highly unique material in figure 9 indicates a high proportion of unique material (usually 40 to 75 percent). Presumably this indicates a strong or specialized collection. The distribution of scarce material in figure 10 indicates a smaller proportion of unique items; nevertheless a large proportion of the collection is composed of material held by three or fewer libraries. Moderate distribution may be characterized by curves of several shapes (two possibilities are shown in figure 11). It indicates that the largest proportion of the collection is composed of materials held by from three to seven institutions. The distribution of common material may be characterized by several shapes (two possibilities are shown in figure 12). It indicates that approximately one-third of the materials are held by five to seven institutions and less than 10 percent are held by eight to ten institutions. The distribution of ubiquitous material may be characterized by curves of several shapes (two possibilities are shown in figure 13). It indicates that at least 10 percent of the material is held by eight to ten institutions.

One interesting area of study was the review of the uniqueness curves by the HEGIS classes. Table 4 reports the distribution among the SUNY libraries. Note that the lowest figure for uniqueness is psychology (47 percent), and that area studies (49 percent) is the only other figure below 50 percent. Note also that the number of titles at the bottom of column two, 47,274, is equal to the number of "actual titles" in the last section of the institution overlap study in table 3.

A review of the "scarce" titles by number and percent for each SUNY institution by HEGIS class is represented in table 5. These data are helpful in program and acquisitions review.

INSTITUTION YCM CORTLAND

SUBCLASS: 0305 African Studies

Total Held in Common With:

$$XBM = 80$$

$$XFM = 33$$

$$YBM = 60$$

$$YGM = 52$$

$$YPM = 44$$

$$YOM = 67$$

$$ZBM = 41$$

$$ZLM = 78$$

$$ZPM = 60$$

$$Total\ Unique = 15$$

Fig. 8. Volumes Cortland Library Holds in Common with Other SUNY Libraries

Conclusions

Work to Date

   A model has been established to describe the library acquisition/retention process, and to support and inform that decision through the manipulation of machine-readable data derived as a byproduct of library, publishing and network operations. Where data are available, programming has been completed to perform disciplinary and overlap analyses on library holdings as recorded on OCLC tapes. Conversion tables from LC to HEGIS have been established.

   A set of data from SUNY campuses have been analyzed through the programs and the results subjected to further review. These subsequent studies to achieve "derived" results were performed by SPSS and manual

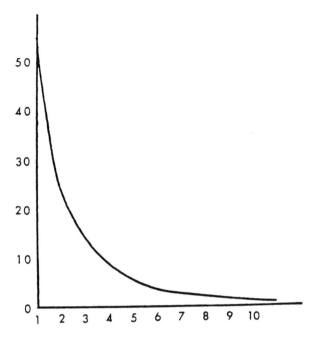

Fig. 9. Graph of Distribution of Highly Unique Material

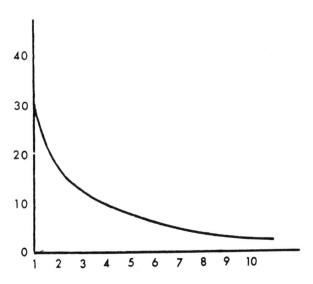

Fig. 10. Graph of Distribution of Scarce Material

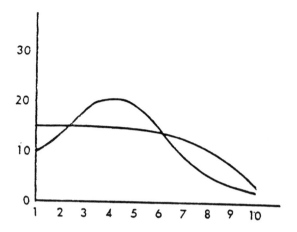

Fig. 11. Graph of Moderate Distribution

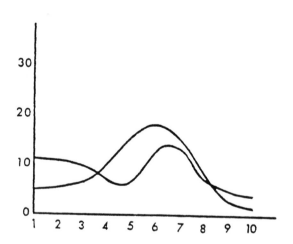

Fig. 12. Graph of Distribution of Common Material

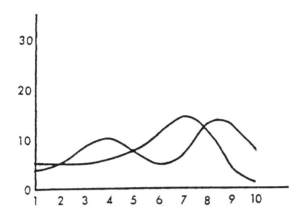

Fig. 13. Graph of Distribution of Ubiquitous Material

analysis, but they are amenable to DSS software when that becomes available.

Study of the results lead to some interesting conclusions. First, there is a very high degree of consonance in the *macrodecisions* made by campuses as they select materials. High correlations between discipline demands and acquisition decisions are observed within each campus. Some disciplines are described as being immanent, that is, they have an inherent relationship between program and acquisition patterns. We do not yet understand why these phenomena occur.

On the other hand, at the *microdecision* (i.e., the decision whether or not to acquire a specific title), remarkable diversity is shown even where programs are apparently similar among campuses. Only two disciplines which have a less than 50 percent uniqueness among ten campuses were found. These results point to four further conclusions:

1. It seems unlikely that an acquisition formula can be defined. It does seem probable that given the data available in this report, plus the incorporation of publishing and price data, a statement which describes the campus academic mission bibliographically can be produced and fine tuned over a period of time and in response to changing circumstance, and provide a firm justification for acquisition budgets.

2. The access system among campuses is essential. All must belong to the same bibliographic network, maintain their database, use the ILL message network, and the same document delivery system. The diversity among the campuses is the greatest bibliographic asset owned by the

university. Easy online access and rapid twenty-four hour delivery of documents is the best possible response to fiscal crises. This is, of course, true of any group of libraries which can display the same characteristics as the SUNY libraries.

3. The bibliographic diversity is a direct result of the subtle diversities of the academic programs at each campus, and a reflection of the book selection processes at each campus. The bibliographic description of the academic mission is a valuable contribution to the academic planning of each campus, and the university as a whole.

4. Although the results reported are based on current acquisitions, the university libraries at SUNY are engaged in retrospective conversion projects. Access to the whole of the bibliographic resource is the natural concomitant of the strategy proposed in number two above.

Planned Developments and Extensions

First, the studies reported in this study must be repeated at a later date to compare the results. The same criteria will be used in the repeat studies. Second, the analysis service is now being offered by SUNY/OCLC as a service to groups of libraries in the state and the country. A number of such analyses have been performed. Their results so far confirm the results reported in this paper. As more results are obtained, SUNY will accumulate them to build a broader picture and perhaps act as a clearinghouse for such studies. Third, Bowker has now announced the availability of its ABPR and BIP files for such projects as the SUNY project. They must be incorporated in the model. Fourth, the serials database in OCLC is growing rapidly. They must be incorporated in the study. Some preliminary studies are promising. Fifth, DSS software must be incorporated to extend the availability and utility of the derived data. Sixth, use data, primarily from OCLC it is anticipated, must be incorporated in the program. Seventh, the U.S. Office of Education has proposed a new and different set of HEGIS codes. Programs must be revised to accept these codes if they are to be accepted by the academic community. We do not have the cost, a time frame, or any sense of the ultimate improvement in the cost efficiency of this step, but if the data produced by the academic institution changes, we have no option. Eighth, ways must found to incorporate the data into academic program planning within institutions. Ninth, the SUNY/OCLC Office of Library Services will seek to extend the utility of the analyses service and acceptance of the reports.

Prognosis

Progress on this project has been very slow. It has been difficult to attract support, increasingly so as the fiscal situation has deteriorated over

TABLE 4
DISTRIBUTION BY HOLDING FREQUENCY OF
1977-78 TITLES HELD BY TEN SUNY COLLEGES
"IN TWO DIGIT HEGIS CLASSES"

	HEGIS Class	*No. of* Titles	*Unique*	2 or Less	3 or Less	5+	8-10
22	Social Sciences	17,499	52%	70%	80%	14%	3.6%
39	Education	10,324	54%	74%	84%	11%	2.5%
15	Letters	8,885	52%	69%	78%	15%	3.3%
21	Public Affairs	7,172	54%	74%	84%	11%	2.7%
05	Business Management	4,316	57%	75%	84%	10%	2.3%
09	Engineering	4,021	62%	81%	90%	6%	0.8%
04	Biological Science	3,893	57%	75%	85%	9%	1.6%
24	Forestry	3,474	61%	79%	87%	8%	1.5%
10	Fine & Applied Arts	3,398	50%	69%	78%	15%	3.5%
11	Foreign Language	3,044	57%	72%	81%	14%	2.5%
20	Psychology	2,716	47%	64%	76%	16%	4.7%
49	Interdisciplinary	2,599	65%	80%	87%	8%	1.2%
13	Home Economics	2,502	52%	71%	80%	13%	4.0%
19	Physical Science	2,329	57%	76%	85%	9%	1.4%
12	Health Professions	1,980	63%	80%	89%	7%	1.5%
14	Law	1,862	75%	88%	92%	5%	1.4%
01	Agriculture	1,628	64%	81%	88%	6%	1.0%
02	Architecture	1,600	65%	80%	88%	8%	1.0%
06	Communications	1,329	50%	66%	77%	17%	3.3%
17	Mathematics	1,257	51%	77%	88%	4%	1.4%
03	Area Studies	1,249	49%	66%	76%	18%	3.2%
16	Library Science	1,116	56%	73%	85%	7%	1.0%
18	Military Science	799	52%	70%	78%	15%	2.7%
07	Computer Info. Sci.	563	62%	80%	91%	4%	1.4%
	Mean (n = 24)		57%	75%	84%	10%	2.2%
	Total Acquisitions	47,274*	54%	72%	81%	12%	2.8%

*Note: Because this table is the result of a component analysis, in which one book may be assigned to more than one discipline, 47,274 is the number of titles assigned to disciplines and is not the sum of all assignments.

TABLE 5
Percent of Scarce Titles and Number of Titles per HEGIS Class by Institution
1977-78 Imprint Dates*

	Brockport	Fredonia	Buffalo	Cortland	Geneseo	Plattsburgh	Oswego	Oneonta	New Paltz	Purchase
22 Social Science	67% 8827	52% 2637	53% 3868	50% 4174	47% 4128	34% 2438	45% 3855	52% 4754	43% 3881	30% 2210
08 Education	74% 5150	44% 1303	58% 2404	64% 2693	47% 2187	38% 1175	51% 2057	57% 2613	45% 1902	33% 574
15 Letters	63% 4127	38% 1409	55% 1860	34% 1484	41% 2060	28% 1255	57% 1976	56% 3216	42% 2383	30% 1329
21 Public Affairs	75% 4012	36% 783	58% 1713	65% 2239	44% 1359	36% 759	49% 1244	56% 1670	41% 1191	29% 527
05 Business/Management	74% 2090	55% 716	59% 883	57% 769	58% 959	43% 534	57% 913	57% 1096	46% 684	29% 312
20 Psychology	69% 1787	26% 383	48% 852	38% 600	36% 650	30% 416	40% 599	43% 796	37% 628	22% 223
49 Inter. Discipline	77% 1099	57% 291	62% 489	64% 476	59% 458	51% 265	62% 562	64% 617	51% 349	40% 223
13 Home Economics	61% 1063	28% 282	61% 824	50% 668	43% 581	34% 302	48% 554	60% 854	40% 501	28% 215
19 Physical Science	71% 894	64% 451	59% 474	50% 274	69% 722	65% 248	61% 582	61% 523	50% 310	38% 174
12 Health Professions	82% 1067	52% 177	61% 318	73% 573	55% 328	56% 197	61% 271	66% 366	45% 241	46% 101
09 Engineering	77% 1401	66% 540	73% 901	69% 565	70% 889	58% 349	68% 880	71% 918	61% 533	48% 244
04 Biological Science	77% 1401	51% 438	63% 762	63% 816	55% 671	49% 549	59% 799	58% 783	49% 612	44% 322

TABLE 5—Continued

	Brockport	Fredonia	Buffalo	Cortland	Geneseo	Plattsburgh	Oswego	Oneonta	New Paltz	Purchase
24 Forestry	81% 1779	54% 355	64% 655	63% 581	61% 592	54% 395	60% 620	61% 734	57% 531	47% 290
10 Fine/Applied Arts	57% 1241	43% 555	51% 797	33% 487	49% 813	21% 435	46% 519	45% 987	52% 1203	54% 1111
11 Foreign Language	72% 1506	44% 488	51% 527	44% 469	43% 502	29% 413	52% 657	52% 904	47% 885	35% 447
14 Law	73% 392	44% 108	74% 357	90% 810	80% 427	24% 92	62% 238	67% 295	43% 143	30% 76
01 Agriculture	76% 634	44% 142	72% 354	68% 307	64% 235	51% 178	65% 316	74% 431	64% 231	41% 111
02 Architecture	82% 808	44% 106	64% 333	61% 207	56% 245	38% 104	61% 271	62% 369	56% 273	57% 214
06 Communication	60% 620	35% 198	50% 362	37% 230	43% 354	27% 198	52% 291	49% 430	48% 425	36% 146
17 Mathematics	87% 831	59% 121	58% 234	31% 94	68% 366	52% 83	70% 322	64% 187	64% 166	25% 32

*Note: The first set of numbers in each case is the percent of titles in the HEGIS class which are scarce (held by three or fewer institutions). The second set is the total number of titles held in the HEGIS class. Thus 67%/8827 indicates that of 8827 titles, 67% are scarce.

the last few years. At the same time, although the service is available, few libraries have taken advantage of it. There is also difficulty in obtaining acceptance and integration of the results into the academic and bibliographic decision-making process. It just takes time and patience.

It is, however, inevitable that, because of their fitness and because of the increased pressures and complexities of decision-making, automated library modeling systems, supported by the analysis of library and other operational data, will gain slow, reluctant acceptance by administrators, budget officials and librarians.

REFERENCES

1. "The Shorter Catechism of Stafford Beer." *Datamation* 28(Feb. 1982):148.

2. Spaulding, F.H., and Stanton, R.O. "Computer-aided Selection in a Library Network." *JASIS* 27(Sept./Oct. 1976):269-80.

3. Keen, Peter G.W. "Information Systems and Organizational Change." *Communications of the Association of Computing Machinery* 24(Jan. 1981):24-33.

4. King, William R. "Using and Evaluating Administrative Decision Support Systems." *New Directions for Higher Education* 35(Sept. 1981):64.

5. Hopkins, David S.P., and Massy, William F. *Planning Models for Colleges and Universities*. Stanford, Calif.: Stanford University Press, 1981, p. 4.

6. King, "Using and Evaluating."

7. Clapp, Verner W., and Jordan, Robert T. "Quantitative Criteria for Adequacy of Academic Library Collections." *College & Research Libraries* 26(Sept. 1965):371-80.

8. New York State Education Department. *Guidelines for Assessing the Adequacy of Academic Libraries in New York State*. Albany, N.Y.: 1976.

9. Evans, Glyn T., et al. *Development of a Responsive Library Acquisitions Formula: Final Report*. Albany, N.Y.: SUNY, Central Administration, 1978.

10. Beazley, Richard M. *Library Statistics of Colleges and Universities: 1979 Institutional Data*. Washington, D.C.: National Center for Educational Statistics, 1981.

11. Beilby, Mary H., and Evans, Glyn T. "An Information System for Collection Development in SUNY: A Progress Report." *Collection Management* 2(Fall 1978):217-28.

12. Huff, Robert A., and Chandler, Marjorie O. *A Taxonomy of Instructional Programs in Higher Education*. Washington, D.C.: National Center for Educational Statistics, 1970.

13. Office of Institutional Research and Analytic Study. *Statistical Abstracts* (Official report produced by the Course and Section Analysis system containing information on instructional workload, faculty, I&DR). Albany, N.Y.: SUNY, OIRAS, 1982.

INDEX